THE ART OF IT MAN

BCS, THE CHARTERED INSTITUTE FOR IT

BCS, The Chartered Institute for IT champions the global IT profession and the interests of individuals engaged in that profession for the benefit of all. We promote wider social and economic progress through the advancement of information technology, science and practice. We bring together industry, academics, practitioners and government to share knowledge, promote new thinking, inform the design of new curricula, shape public policy and inform the public.

Our vision is to be a world-class organisation for IT. Our 70,000 strong membership includes practitioners, businesses, academics and students in the UK and internationally. We deliver a range of professional development tools for practitioners and employees. A leading IT qualification body, we offer a range of widely recognised qualifications.

Further Information
BCS, The Chartered Institute for IT,
First Floor, Block D,
North Star House, North Star Avenue,
Swindon, SN2 1FA, United Kingdom.
T +44 (0) 1793 417 424
F +44 (0) 1793 417 444
www.bcs.org/contact

http://shop.bcs.org/

THE ART OF IT MANAGEMENT
Practical tools, techniques and people skills

Robina Chatham

Published by BCS Learning & Development Ltd, a wholly owned subsidiary of BCS, The Chartered Institute for IT, First Floor, Block D, North Star House, North Star Avenue, Swindon, SN2 1FA, UK.
www.bcs.org

Paperback ISBN: 978-1-78017-290-3
PDF ISBN: 978-1-78017-291-0
ePUB ISBN: 978-1-78017-292-7
Kindle ISBN: 978-1-78017-293-4

Ebook available

British Cataloguing in Publication Data.
A CIP catalogue record for this book is available at the British Library.

Disclaimer:
The views expressed in this book are of the author(s) and do not necessarily reflect the views of the Institute or BCS Learning & Development Ltd except where explicitly stated as such. Although every care has been taken by the author(s) and BCS Learning & Development Ltd in the preparation of the publication, no warranty is given by the author(s) or BCS Learning & Development Ltd as publisher as to the accuracy or completeness of the information contained within it and neither the author(s) nor BCS Learning & Development Ltd shall be responsible or liable for any loss or damage whatsoever arising by virtue of such information or any instructions or advice contained within this publication or by any of the aforementioned.

BCS books are available at special quantity discounts to use as premiums and sale promotions, or for use in corporate training programmes. Please visit our Contact us page at www.bcs.org/contact

Typeset by Lapiz Digital Services, Chennai, India.

Printed and bound in Great Britain by Henry Ling Limited at the Dorset Press, Dorchester DT1 1HD

CONTENTS

List of figures and tables ix
About the author x
Foreword xi
Acknowledgements xii
Preface xiii

PART 1 ESSENTIAL MANAGEMENT SKILLS **1**

1. WHAT MAKES A GOOD MANAGER? **3**
 Why is this important? 3
 Delving a little deeper into the subject 3
 Hints and tips 5
 Reference 8

2. HOW TO DELEGATE EFFECTIVELY **9**
 Why is this important? 9
 Delving a little deeper into the subject 10
 Hints and tips 10

3. GIVING AND RECEIVING FEEDBACK **15**
 Why is this important? 15
 Delving a little deeper into the subject 15
 Hints and tips 17

4. DEALING WITH POOR PERFORMANCE **21**
 Why is this important? 21
 Delving a little deeper into the subject 21
 Hints and tips 23

5. DEVELOPING TEAMS **28**
 Why is this important? 28
 Delving a little deeper into the subject 28
 Hints and tips 30
 Reference 32

6. CHANGE LEADERSHIP **33**
 Why is this important? 33
 Delving a little deeper into the subject 33
 Hints and tips 35
 References 37

7.	THINKING STRATEGICALLY	38
	Why is this important?	38
	Delving a little deeper into the subject	38
	Hints and tips	39

PART 2 SKILLS THAT YOU HAVE ALWAYS NEEDED BUT ARE NOW MORE CRITICAL — 43

8.	EFFECTIVE COMMUNICATION	45
	Why is this important?	45
	Delving a little deeper into the subject	45
	Hints and tips	47

9.	THE ART OF INFLUENCING	53
	Why is this important?	53
	Delving a little deeper into the subject	53
	Hints and tips	54
	Reference	55

10.	REPORTS AND PRESENTATIONS	56
	Why is this important?	56
	Delving a little deeper into the subject	56
	Hints and tips	56

11.	UNDERSTANDING YOUR CUSTOMERS	63
	Why is this important?	63
	Delving a little deeper into the subject	63
	Hints and tips	64

12.	MANAGING AND NEGOTIATING WITH SUPPLIERS	67
	Why is this important?	67
	Delving a little deeper into the subject	67
	Hints and tips	67

13.	MANAGING YOUR BOSS	70
	Why is this important?	70
	Delving a little deeper into the subject	71
	Hints and tips	71

14.	RELATIONSHIP MANAGEMENT	75
	Why is this important?	75
	Delving a little deeper into the subject	75
	Hints and tips	77

PART 3 THINGS THAT YOU NEED TO UNDERSTAND, HAVE AN OPINION ON AND MAKE A CONTRIBUTION TO — 79

15.	SYSTEMS AND PROCESSES	81
	Why is this important?	81
	Delving a little deeper into the subject	81
	Hints and tips	82

16. THE EXPLODING IMPACT OF IT IN THE DIGITAL ERA 86
Why is this important? 86
Delving a little deeper into the subject 86
Hints and tips 87
Reference 88

PART 4 THINGS THAT MAY BE KEEPING YOU AWAKE AT NIGHT 89

17. MANAGING PEOPLE WHO USED TO BE A PEER, OR
WHO ARE OLDER OR MORE EXPERIENCED THAN YOU 91
Why is this important? 91
Delving a little deeper into the subject 91
Hints and tips 92

18. LETTING GO OF THE THINGS THAT YOU SHOULD NO LONGER BE
DOING YOURSELF 94
Why is this important? 94
Delving a little deeper into the subject 94
Hints and tips 94

19. COPING WITH STRESS AND PRESSURE 96
Why is this important? 96
Delving a little deeper into the subject 96
Hints and tips 97

20. ACHIEVING A SATISFYING WORK/LIFE BALANCE 100
Why is this important? 100
Delving a little deeper into the subject 100
Hints and tips 103

21. MANAGING AND ENHANCING YOUR REPUTATION 107
Why is this important? 107
Delving a little deeper into the subject 107
Hints and tips 108

22. HOW TO DEAL WITH ORGANISATIONAL POLITICS 113
Why is this important? 113
Delving a little deeper into the subject 114
Hints and tips 116

23. MY BOSS IS A BULLY – HOW DO I COPE? 120
Why is this important? 120
Delving a little deeper into the subject 120
Hints and tips 122

PART 5 TOOLS THAT WILL HELP — **125**

24. **HOW TO MANAGE YOUR TIME TO MAXIMUM EFFECT** — **127**
Why is this important? — 127
Delving a little deeper into the subject — 127
Hints and tips — 128
Reference — 131

25. **DEVELOPING YOUR EMOTIONAL INTELLIGENCE** — **132**
Why is this important? — 132
Delving a little deeper into the subject — 132
Hints and tips — 133

26. **HOW TO ENGENDER TRUST AND LOYALTY FROM OTHERS** — **142**
Why is this important? — 142
Delving a little deeper into the subject — 142
Hints and tips — 143
Reference — 144

27. **HOW TO MANAGE YOUR PERSONAL DEVELOPMENT** — **145**
Why is this important? — 145
Delving a little deeper into the subject — 145
Hints and tips — 146

28. **COACHING SKILLS** — **148**
Why is this important? — 148
Delving a little deeper into the subject — 148
Hints and tips — 149

29. **THE IMPORTANCE OF MAINTAINING A SENSE OF HUMOUR** — **153**
Why is this important? — 153
Delving a little deeper into the subject — 153
Hints and tips — 154

30. **FINAL WORDS** — **156**

APPENDIX: YOUR FIRST 90 DAYS AS A NEW MANAGER — **158**
Preparation — 158
Making a start — 159
Putting it all together — 160
The finale — 161
Additional hints and tips — 162
Taking stock – the IT health check — 162
IT health check questionnaire — 163
Scoring key — 166
Benchmark — 166

FURTHER READING — **168**

Index — 172

LIST OF FIGURES AND TABLES

Figure 2.1	Skill versus will matrix	11
Figure 4.1	Performance portfolio	22
Figure 6.1	Behaviour through the change curve	34
Figure 8.1	Communication needs	46
Figure 10.1	Style of presentation for the pragmatic types	57
Figure 10.2	Style of presentation for the theoretical types	58
Figure 10.3	Style of presentation for the idealistic types	59
Figure 10.4	Style of presentation for the sociable types	60
Figure 15.1	Project portfolio	83
Figure 16.1	Harnessing the potential of IT	87
Figure 17.1	People skills, qualities and attributes	92
Figure 19.1	Effects of stress on performance	97
Figure 20.1	Maslow's hierarchy of needs	102
Figure 20.2	Work/life balance triangle	103
Figure 21.1	Your personal brand	111
Figure 22.1	The political zoo	115
Figure 23.1	Types of bully	121
Figure 24.1	Priority matrix	128
Figure A.1	Systems analysis	161
Figure A.2	Prioritising opportunities	162
Figure A.3	Example output from an IT health check	164
Figure A.4	IT health check questionnaire	165
Figure A.5	Scoring key for IT health check	166
Figure A.6	IT health check – benchmarking data	167
Table 3.1	Helpful and unhelpful feedback	19
Table 19.1	Dos and don'ts of dealing with others under stress	99
Table 20.1	List of values	104

ABOUT THE AUTHOR

Dr Robina Chatham has over 30 years experience in IT. Positions that she has held range from project manager within the shipbuilding industry to European CIO for a merchant bank and lecturer at Cranfield School of Management. She is qualified as both a mechanical engineer and a neuroscientist. Previous books include *Corporate politics for IT managers: How to get streetwise*; *Changing the IT leader's mindset: Time for revolution rather than evolution* and *30 key questions that unlock management: How do I...?*

Robina now runs her own company specialising in management development and executive coaching. She is also a visiting fellow at Cranfield School of Management. Her prime focus is on helping senior managers to develop political acumen, master the art of influencing others and hence increase their personal impact at board level. Other areas of specialism include the building of high performance teams and relationship management. She has considerable international experience and regularly speaks at both academic and professional conferences worldwide.

FOREWORD

The Art of IT Management is the start to creating or extending competitive advantage – a must read!

IT is now core to improving every function in a company from simple electronic employee payroll deposits to the most complex business processes. An average IT department will yield average performance results; however, if a company aspires to leadership, exceptional IT is a requirement. Technology can only get you so far; it's the IT employees who bring technical solutions to life and create value through business process transformation, solution development and daily operational excellence. These are weighty tasks that make the IT manager role critical to the success of any company.

Transition into management is one of the most challenging career steps an IT professional makes. In *The Art of IT Management*, Robina offers practical advice to help managers create an environment of mutual trust, respect and fulfilling work that helps IT employees and managers achieve their career best performance. The real life stories and advice she shares provide new IT managers with a great resource for successfully working through situations they'll inevitably face, and gives experienced managers solid insights into looking to improve their teams' results.

IT managers are agents of change for the company; yet, this is rarely included in the job description. As an IT manager, you have the responsibility to implement business process changes, help set direction on strategic changes and ensure your employees have the skill-set needed to keep pace with technology. *The Art of IT Management* explains how IT professionals can position themselves as positive catalysts for change.

Robina understands that IT management is about personal growth and requires the acknowledgement that the skills that got you here are not the skills that will continue to propel your career forward. This book is a great resource for both new and experienced managers to deliver transformative business results and, in doing so, propel their careers forward.

Kim Stevenson
Corporate Vice President and
Chief Information Officer
Intel Corporation

ACKNOWLEDGEMENTS

I would like to give a huge vote of thanks to Neil Williams who has been my rock through the writing of this book. Neil, your encouragement, wisdom and insights have been invaluable and added much to the substance of these works. I would also like to thank Erika Maass for the many hours she has spent reading this text, for her diligence, foresight and meticulous feedback. My thanks also go to Tracey Masters for reading and commenting on various parts of this text and for inspiring me in my moments of despondency.

I am most grateful to Kim Stevenson for her encouragement and for providing the foreword to this book. My publishers also deserve a big thank you for their helpful feedback and meticulous editing.

My appreciation goes to my friend and colleague, Stephen Carver, for the flight and aircraft analogy used in Chapter 15. Stephen, without your guidance and vision, this chapter would be but a pale shadow of its current form.

My husband, John Carrington, has earned a massive thank you too for his patience and understanding, for coping with my frustrations and for keeping me fed and watered whilst I was distracted in my writing pursuits.

Last, but by no means least, I would like to thank Syd (the cat) who has kept me entertained during my many hours alone attempting to artfully craft meaningful words. He has a passion for lying on my keyboard, and in the process, has managed to delete huge swathes of text on a number of occasions, but I still love him.

PREFACE

This book has been written primarily for IT managers just stepping into their first managerial position; however, many more seasoned IT managers and leaders will also benefit from this text. For some it may prove a useful refresher, for others it may fill a vital gap in their portfolio of knowledge or provide that 'light bulb' moment of revelation.

Most IT professionals who find themselves in a management position for the first time are ill prepared and hence may feel a little lost. Management is about people rather than process or procedure. You need the knowledge and know-how to show people the way, the vision to know where you are going, the passion to take people with you and the ability to empathise with individuals. Management is therefore an art rather than a science. There is no one particular right way; every situation you face as a manager will have an element of uniqueness. Your approach, therefore, has to be geared to the person concerned, the task in hand, their level of skill and maturity, their attitude and aptitude and so on.

This book will provide you with some theory and some tools and techniques, but, unlike many other books, its focus is on practical advice. You will find hints and tips, case studies, stories and examples from the world of IT. Many of the skills described in this book are generic management capabilities. What makes this book different and unique is that it has been written for the person with a scientific mind and a technical background; for someone who is undoubtedly highly intelligent with an enquiring mind, but may not be so capable in their dealings with people.

This book has been written from personal experience, I was a first time IT manager once. Although I studied mechanical engineering at University, I found I had a natural aptitude for building relationships with, and getting the best out of, people; hence I was rapidly promoted. By the age of 34 I held my first head of IT position, managing more than 70 people. Two years later I was the European CIO for a merchant bank. I have, therefore, 'been there, done that and got the T-shirt'. For the past 19 years I have been engaged in the business of management development and executive coaching, primarily within the IT community. I have learned how people learn, what works and what doesn't work. All the stories you will read in this book are true; all the advice has been personally tried and tested; all the tools and techniques have been road tested by other aspiring leaders who have gone before you with positive results.

If you are a new manager I would recommend that you read this book cover to cover. As you gain more experience you may want to dip and dive as you come across certain situations and face various challenges. If you are a more seasoned manager start with the contents page and read those chapters of particular relevance or interest to you. I would challenge any IT leader or manager, no matter how experienced, not to take something away from this book, in particular Part 5. So, grab a comfy chair, sit back, relax, read and enjoy!

Finally, I wish you all the best in your current role and all your roles to come.

PART 1
ESSENTIAL MANAGEMENT SKILLS

1   WHAT MAKES A GOOD MANAGER?

WHY IS THIS IMPORTANT?

In the world of information technology (IT) many people get promoted to a managerial position because they are good at their job and that job is likely to be a technical one. However, being a manager is very different from being a 'doer'. Often people are expected to rise to the challenge with little training, guidance or preparation and, just to make it even more difficult, they may also be expected to manage former 'work mates'. No wonder the result is often described as 'losing a good technician and gaining a poor manager'.

A manager's role is to get the best out of their staff, as individual members and also as a collective team. There are many definitions of management/leadership; my favourite one is 'Consistently achieving results beyond expectations by creating a climate in which others can shine' (Fellows, 2012).

People work best when they feel good about themselves, have interesting work to do and when they are afforded a sense of job satisfaction and the opportunity for growth and/or advancement. Research by Cass Business School suggests that:

- 6% of people like to be told what to do;
- 4% of people prefer complete freedom;
- 90% of people respond best to freedom within guidelines.

As a manager your job is to provide the guidelines, but make sure there is freedom within. If you are too prescriptive your staff will lose any sense of job satisfaction, will become demotivated and will give you the bare minimum at best. You need to give enough, but not too much, guidance and support; this will differ with each member of your team. You must never do your staff's job for them – you need to keep your eyes open, but your hands off – and you need to ask the right questions rather than providing the 'right' answers.

DELVING A LITTLE DEEPER INTO THE SUBJECT

When asked the question 'what do you consider to be the main qualities of a leader?' the most common answers are:

- strong character;
- charismatic;

- possesses great personal drive;
- intelligent;
- decisive;
- courageous;
- ability to be ruthless when necessary;
- confident.

However, when asked to think about one's own boss(es) and what leadership qualities are appreciated most, the answers are very different:

- sense of humour;
- unpretentious;
- knowledgeable;
- empathetic and supportive;
- good listener;
- honest and trustworthy;
- prepared to admit mistakes;
- consistent.

The two lists above are quite different in nature – the first is all about self and the second more about your impact on others. This shows that management is all about your impact on others and about getting people to do what is asked of them, not because they are forced to, but because they want to.

As a manager there are five simple rules that will help you get the best out of your staff and establish your credibility as their leader:

- **Treat people well.** Be fair, be considerate, be compassionate and be inspirational. Treat people as individuals; learn what each member of your team responds best to in terms of communication style, motivational techniques and feedback and reward mechanisms. You will find more on this in Chapters 3 and 8.

- **Get the instructions right.** Make sure that you have communicated clearly and effectively; check for understanding. Ensure your people know exactly what is expected of them, by when and how their performance will be measured and judged. There should be a minimum standard that every member of your team will be required to meet. However, goals should be geared towards an individual; they should be achievable, but also stretch the person (see Chapter 2 for more on this subject).

- **Motivate and inspire your people.** Make sure that whatever you have delegated is sufficiently stretching and challenging, but within a person's capability. People should, on balance, find their work interesting. If this is not the case you need to find out why and be prepared to make some role adjustments. Look for opportunities to praise, encourage, reward and provide constructive feedback.

Be approachable and make yourself available to offer guidance when required. Take a personal interest in your team members and make your people feel good about themselves. Maintain a sense of humour – especially when things go wrong. You will find more on this subject in Chapters 3 and 4.

- **Let them get on with it.** Allow people the freedom to do things their way. Focus on outcomes rather than the means of achieving those outcomes. Never ever take a task back. Ask questions to stimulate thought processes. If appropriate provide data, but not answers, and if necessary open doors or remove obstacles (see Chapter 2 for more on this).

- **Demonstrate your value.** Many IT professionals do not have much respect or regard for the managerial role. They do not see its purpose or function. Another factor to consider is that as you become more focused on management activities you also become more distant from your technical roots and may find yourself managing people who know more than you do about the technical aspects of their job. But you still need to earn their respect. You will find guidance and examples of how you may achieve this in the following section.

HINTS AND TIPS

You might not be able to compete with your team technically, but you can value their technical expertise and take an interest in what they are doing. Similarly, they need to value your managerial skills and the role you perform.

The following list outlines the things that **you should be doing**:

- Have a plan – i.e. be clear in your own mind what you want, when you want it and in what form you want it – and ensure that you have communicated it well; ensure that all your actions are consistent with that plan.

- Build effective relationships with your team:

  - Take an interest in them as people – I do not mean that you need to know what they did last Saturday evening, but you should know the names and rough ages of their children and you should know where they have just been on holiday and ask them how it was.

  - Take an interest in their work but do not do it for them.

  - Develop the ability to have conversations on a wide range of subjects.

  - Find common ground of mutual interest.

- Ensure that your people have the tools, resources and necessary training to do the things you ask of them. Resolve external issues that may impede their performance – fight the battles for them. If, for example, a member of your team is struggling to get the cooperation they need from another department, go and see the manager from that department and clear the path for them. For more information on this, see Chapter 22 on organisational politics.

- Delegate by talking about desired outcomes, rather than being prescriptive as to how those outcomes should be achieved. See Chapter 2 for more on delegation.

- Look for opportunities to praise – be specific. 'I really liked the way you handled that situation when ...', 'I thought your conclusions were spot on in your analysis of ...' and so on. See Chapter 3 for more on giving feedback.

- Ensure your team take the credit for your successes and open doors for them to demonstrate their capabilities in more senior circles. See Chapter 4 for more on developing your people.

- Be open and honest and true to your values.

- Ensure that you address their needs at all levels:

  - Physical needs – people do not work effectively if they are too hot or cold, uncomfortable or in poor lighting conditions.

  - Personal needs – you will need to make allowances for your people's personal circumstances and commitments. If they are worried about being able to pick a child up on time or a sick relative left alone, their mind will not be focused on the job. This is always a fine balance: you need to be fair and reasonable from both the organisation's and the individual's perspective. You need to think how you would like to be dealt with if you were in their place. Mostly, good judgement comes with experience. If you have a mentor this may be a good time to seek their guidance.

  - Motivational needs – different things motivate different people. It could be the opportunity for promotion, public recognition, the opportunity to learn or a pat on the back. You need to find out what works for each member of your team. You will find more on this subject in Chapter 3.

  - Development needs – to keep people interested they need variety and to be stretched. Think how you could enhance their role; what other aspects of your role could you delegate? What training would they benefit from and where would coaching be more appropriate? Again, you will find more on this subject in Chapter 3.

  - Aspirational needs – few people want to perform the same role for the rest of their working lives. Find out what each individual member of your team would like to be doing in one year and five years. What could you do to help them on their journey? See Chapter 4 for more on developing your people.

- Let there be laughter in the office – people are more productive when they are happy and having a little fun.

- Never forget that you are the boss and that you do have the right to tell one of your team to do something or not. Sometimes you will have to get tough just like a parent has to with a naughty child – respect runs both ways. See Chapter 25 for more on conflict resolution.

- Be fair and equitable while also treating people as individuals.

Demonstrate your value through action by doing things for your people that they could never hope to achieve themselves. Such supportive actions will also help you to build mutual trust. The following mini case illustrates this point nicely.

George is a middle manager working in the IT department of a retail bank. The IT department underwent a major reorganisation and in his new role, George inherited a team of 17 very intelligent and highly skilled 'super techies'. These people were exceedingly independent and had the reputation of being 'unmanageable'. They viewed their own management as a hindrance rather than a help.

George was well aware that he needed to make an immediate impact and create a positive impression in the eyes of his new team. He also needed to demonstrate the value of his managerial position. His predecessor had had a tough time, being ignored, side-lined and sniped at, and although his predecessor was not a bad guy, he had never established his worth in the eyes of his team.

Within a few weeks, George had them 'eating out of his hand', talking to him, asking for his help on various political issues, involving him and doing anything he asked of them. How did he achieve this?

As everyone knows, reorganisations generally involve a physical component, i.e. where people sit. There was one particularly sought-after area within the large and essentially open-plan office; it was a south-facing window location that was somewhat 'off the beaten track'. Everyone wanted to sit there and, predictably, the most competitive of George's colleagues acquired this space for his team. At their level of management, George's entire peer group had their own offices dotted around the big open-plan area and although responsibilities were changing, status was not; therefore, none of them was required or expected to move office. George played on his competitive colleague's weakness – his ego – and offered to swap his own larger office for his colleague's smaller one in exchange for the best physical location for his team. George instantly won his team's respect and admiration. He never told them how he had achieved this feat, but merely quipped that it was 'for him to know and them to wonder'. It was at this point that they started to understand what the role of a manager was all about and how George could be of use to them.

The following list outlines the things that **you should not be doing**:

- Do not be tempted to do any member of your team's job for them even if you could do it quicker and better yourself. Never ever take a job back and do not micro-manage. On the opposite side of the equation, neither should you abdicate responsibility – you must monitor progress and maintain an interest in their work. You will find more on this subject in Chapter 2.

- Do not be too prescriptive of how they should achieve a certain task. Leave room for creativity and give people the opportunity to do it their own way.

- Do not look for opportunities to criticise.

- Do not blame your team when things go wrong; you can delegate authority, but you cannot delegate accountability.

- Do not shut them out, or overtly take the credit for their successes.

- Never ever say one thing, but then do another – make sure your words and deeds are congruent.

- Never lie to your team – it will destroy all trust. If you cannot tell them something because you have been bound by secrecy, then tell them you cannot tell them. Do not deny something is happening when it is – remember the rumour mill is a very powerful and surprisingly accurate source of information.

- Do not try to be one of the 'lads' or 'lasses', but neither should you be aloof and distant. See Chapter 17 for more on moving from team mate to team leader.

- Do not expect your staff to read your mind. Communicate clearly and check for understanding to ensure the message has been received as you intended.

- Do not ever play one team member off against another.

- Never be critical or give negative feedback to a member of your team in the presence of another person. You can tackle them in private, but always support them in public.

As time progresses you will move further away from your technical roots, it therefore becomes even more important for you to demonstrate your leadership capability and what a manager contributes to the team that the team members cannot.

REFERENCE

Fellows, D. (2012) Leadership and management. In: *Charity Technology Conference*. London, November 2012. London: Cass Business School, Centre for Charity Effectiveness. Session 7.

2   HOW TO DELEGATE EFFECTIVELY

WHY IS THIS IMPORTANT?

Delegation is about giving up part of your job with three prime objectives:

- growing your subordinates;
- creating space in your own diary so that your boss can delegate part of their job to you;
- allowing yourself time to develop into your new role and, as time progresses, develop that role.

As a manager your organisational value lies not in what you can do, but rather what you can enable others to do; this is rooted in your ability to delegate.

In all my 33 years of experience working within IT functions and consulting to them, I find that the vast majority of junior to middle managers have far too much to do; they feel stressed that they cannot keep up with all the demands on their time and seldom leave the office at the appointed hour. In contrast, in many cases, their staff have too little planned work to do and hence plenty of time to indulge in perfectionism, experimentation, creating new features and other 'off-piste' activities. When delegation does take place, IT managers often strike the wrong balance between task and people focus; between freedom and control.

All managers have a duty to develop their people so that they can achieve their full potential and, in so doing, contribute to the broader business success. This element of the manager's role is a form of organisational stewardship that requires a level of selflessness and a willingness to see the key role of management as developing people.

Managers who fail to delegate or who delegate poorly are failing their organisation and failing in a duty of care to their people. Failure to delegate appropriately will lead to:

- people not realising their talents and underperforming;
- people not knowing what they are supposed to be doing;
- people working at cross purposes or in general confusion;
- missed deadlines, increased stress and, ultimately, burn-out;

- a vacuum when you need to move on and no one has the skills to succeed you. Indeed one of the biggest issues that organisations face today at all levels of management is succession.

DELVING A LITTLE DEEPER INTO THE SUBJECT

Understanding why managers avoid delegation, or fail to do it well, is the first step towards developing your own abilities. There are three principal psychological barriers to delegation:

- It often involves giving up jobs that you like doing – this is the difference between being efficient and being effective. You may scrub floors efficiently, but being effective is about directing your efforts to the right job.

- It usually involves overcoming the fear of losing control – people tend to think (sometimes rightly) that nobody else can do the job as well as them. When they give a task to someone, they then unfairly judge the quality of what is produced and often end up redoing all or part of it to their own exacting standards. This creates needless extra work and stress that could have been avoided.

- There is a need to balance two, potentially competing, psychological contracts – one with your own leadership or customer who wants the outcome of your delegated task and the other with the person you delegated the task to. These contracts tend to be implicit rather than explicit and people are often lax at making sure that everyone's expectations are aligned. You might find it helpful at this point to reread the five simple rules in Chapter 1.

In addition to the psychological barriers, there is also the practical barrier that delegation takes time and effort. You need to select the right person, brief them properly, spend extra time guiding their efforts and reviewing their progress, and finally you need to check their output. This all takes time and effort and unless you create the time and space to do it properly, the chances are that your efforts will simply result in frustration and confusion.

Even when you manage to overcome the psychological and practical barriers that stop most managers from delegating effectively, you are still faced with the issue of organisational responsibility. You need to remember that you can delegate tasks and the authority to do those tasks, but you cannot delegate accountability. You are the manager. If it all goes wrong you are accountable because you have managed unwisely. Pointing downwards and claiming 'the dumb cluck let me down' is just another way of saying 'I'm a poor manager who doesn't know how to manage people and can't see what is happening around me'. The buck stops with you – if you delegate and someone messes up, that someone is you.

HINTS AND TIPS

Delegation is an art rather than a science. It requires common sense, compassion, courage and a genuine concern for the well-being and growth of your people. If you possess all these attributes, with a little practice you will become a great manager.

It is important to remember that there is no one-size-fits-all approach. You need to evaluate the person to whom you have chosen to delegate. First, consider if they have the skills and knowledge to do the task and, second, consider if they have the desire to take the task on. Use the skill/will matrix in Figure 2.1 to assess how you should approach and manage each potential delegatee.

Figure 2.1 Skill versus will matrix

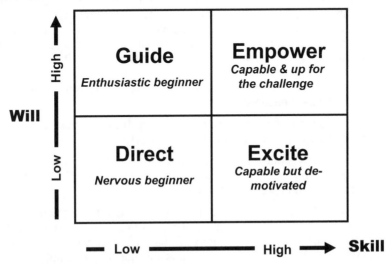

Direct those with low skill and low will – If your delegatee has neither the skill nor the will to do the task, your style of management needs to be directive i.e. prescriptive. You should start with relatively straightforward, well-bounded tasks that are likely to recur soon so that they can get additional practice at the same sort of activity. You will need to:

- Start with the outcome: paint a clear picture of what needs to be achieved and how success will be measured.

- Explain in reasonable detail how they should approach the task, but be flexible if they come up with any acceptable alternatives.

- Check their understanding by asking them to explain, in their words, what you have just told them.

- Provide clear guidelines: make sure that constraints and boundaries are explained. Advise them of the minimum standard required. Ensure that they have access to any information needed.

- Work backwards from the deadline: if the output is needed by close of business next Friday, you need to set a deadline of close of business next Wednesday. Remember, they probably have not done this before and so they will need more time, and you will need time to check and possibly polish the output.

- Give them just enough training as they are about to take on the task and top up as required.

- Supervise closely and provide frequent feedback against progress. Look for opportunities to praise, encourage and excite.

- On completion, celebrate and reward their success.

- Never, ever, be tempted to take the job back.

Guide those with low skill and high will – If your delegatee has the will but not the skill, your style of management needs to be one of guidance. Such people are ready and eager for a challenge but do not have the skills and knowledge required to perform well. They probably do not realise how little they know and in their eagerness are likely to charge into things and make mistakes – mistakes that they may not recognise and that may have serious consequences. They still need lots of direction, but you will need to be subtle about how you provide this as they tend to be impatient. You will need to:

- Start with the outcome: paint a clear picture of what needs to be achieved and how success will be measured.

- Suggest in broad terms how they may go about the task and ask them to bring back a detailed plan of action before they start work.

- Check their plan and confirm their understanding of what outcomes need to be produced and advise them of the minimum required standard. Ensure that they have access to any information needed.

- Work backwards from the deadline: if the output is needed by close of business next Friday, you need to set a deadline of close of business next Wednesday. Remember, they probably have not done this before and so they will need more time and you will need time to check and possibly polish the output.

- Temper their enthusiasm by asking them to think through what might go wrong and where they may need help.

- Give them just enough training as they are about to take on the task and top up as required. Identify people they can talk to who have done something similar.

- Monitor their progress and provide feedback as appropriate. Look for opportunities to praise and encourage.

- On completion, celebrate and reward their success.

- Never, ever, be tempted to take the job back.

By adopting this approach, you will be able to control without demotivating and de-risk the situation while learning takes place and mistakes are likely. As progress is made you will be able to relax the frequency and depth of your controls.

Excite those with high skill and low will – If your delegatee has the skill but not the will to do the task, your style of management needs to excite. Such people are well able to do the required task, but are reluctant to step up to the plate. They may have had a previous bad experience or may not have learned to trust you. They may be bored and not sufficiently stretched. Managers often ignore or side-line these sorts of people as being too difficult. However, these are key resources and need to be engaged for their benefit, for the benefit of the team and for the benefit of the organisation. You will need to:

- Start with the outcome: paint a clear picture of what needs to be achieved and how success will be measured.

- Encourage them by telling them what you think of their capabilities and explain why you feel they are well suited to the task.

- Explore the reason for their reluctant attitude. Is it a question of your management style, or some previous bad experience? Are they bored, in the wrong job or is some personal factor getting in the way? Find out what motivates them and what aspects of their job that they do enjoy.

- Energise and engage them: use them as a sounding board for ideas, show them that you value their input and include them in scoping the task and defining the outputs and quality criteria to be used.

- Ensure that they have access to any information needed and that there are no barriers to impede their progress.

- Develop a coaching relationship, with the objective being their personal growth. Remember that the relationship between coach and coachee must be elective and trust based (see Chapter 28 for more on coaching).

- Set them goals that will stretch their capability, monitor their progress and provide frequent feedback. Look for opportunities to praise, encourage and excite.

- Ensure that they get wider recognition for their efforts – involve them in presentations to clients or senior leaders. Sing their praises to the rest of the team and your boss and peers. Celebrate and reward their success.

Empower those with high skill and high will – If your delegatee has the skill and the will to do the task then your style of management needs to be one of empowerment. Such people are ready and eager for the challenge. If you do not harness their energy, they will probably find a way to go around you. These are candidates for your succession planning. You should go beyond just delegating tasks to these people – you need to delegate decision-making also as this is a key management skill. You will need to:

- Talk about the desired outcomes and ask them how they would achieve them.

- Use analytical and explorative questions to check that they have considered every angle in relation to the problem or opportunity.

- Involve them in decision-making and the identification of additional resources or information required. Ask them to identify any barriers that may impede their progress.

- Give them the responsibility for getting other people up to speed and fulfil any training needs.

- Adopt a coaching style in order to grow your 'star performer' (see Chapter 28 for more on coaching).

- Look for opportunities to praise and encourage. Do not ignore them and do not over-manage them.

- On completion, celebrate and reward their success.

Whatever your staff's skill or will, remember that it is your job to open any doors that need to be opened so that they have access to the people and resources that they will need. Inform others what is going on so that they can help facilitate timely access to people and information.

Take your hands off, but keep your eyes open; be approachable and make yourself available for advice or guidance when required. Gain pleasure and job satisfaction through watching your staff grow and develop as a result of your nurturing efforts.

3 GIVING AND RECEIVING FEEDBACK

WHY IS THIS IMPORTANT?

Everyone needs feedback, but few people either give or receive enough. On balance, everyone is in need of a little more than they are prepared to give.

Feedback is important for people's learning and development, to boost morale and send them home feeling valued and motivated to take on even bigger challenges. Feedback takes two prime forms, formal and informal. Informal feedback is the comments and suggestions you make about people's work on a day-by-day basis. Formal feedback is the process you follow as prescribed by an organisational procedure. Such procedures are normally laid down by the human resources (HR) function.

Formal feedback should be no surprise if informal feedback has been done regularly, consistently and properly. However, this is often not the case and hence formal mechanisms are put in place to ensure that some feedback is given at least periodically. The catch-22 is that if managers do not engage in informal feedback, the annual appraisal process becomes all the more difficult. If you find the informal process a challenge, then the formal annual interview and report will be an even more daunting prospect.

Equally, you need to consider your own position: how good is your own boss at giving feedback to you? If your boss is unskilled in giving you feedback, you have two choices. You can either accept your fate and hope that things improve in the future or you can take action by asking your manager for feedback and making it easy for them to provide it (more on this in the next section).

Feedback from your boss is important, but should not be your only source. Encourage and ask for feedback from your staff, your peers, your customers and even your suppliers. This is often referred to as 360 degree feedback, which again can be both formal and informal.

DELVING A LITTLE DEEPER INTO THE SUBJECT

Giving feedback

It is not uncommon for technical managers with their logical minds to feel that their staff should know if they have done a good job and therefore do not need to be told what they already know. On the opposite side of the equation technical managers can be quick to criticise or point out mistakes, but seldom do this in a constructive manner. Alternatively, they may moan to others about their unhappiness regarding certain events or behaviours, but fail to tackle the situation with the person concerned.

As a manager of people, part of your role is to create a climate for a regular, open exchange on performance, to praise and encourage when appropriate and to discuss areas in need of improvement.

The way in which you give feedback should communicate acceptance of the recipient as a worthwhile person and an acceptance of their right to be different and do things their way (providing they have achieved the overall objective). You can be critical of their work output or behaviours, but never of them as a person.

The following mini case study provides a positive illustration of how feedback should be given.

Bob was a particularly intelligent, committed and well-liked member of his team and had a history of very positive appraisals and promises of promotion and pay rises. The promotion and pay rises had, however, never materialised. He became confused and disillusioned and the rest of the team was very much on his side. A new manager took it upon herself to find out why this apparent anomaly existed and address the problem.

Part of Bob's role was to 'police' technical standards and he inevitably had to say 'no' from time to time; in the process he had upset a few powerful individuals and been accused of having a somewhat brusque manner and cutting sense of humour.

Bob's previous manager had ducked the issue. Bob had received little informal feedback and at appraisal time his manager had simply focused on Bob's positive attributes and told Bob what he wanted to hear, effectively sweeping the issues under the carpet. By contrast, Bob's new manager was totally open and honest with him about her findings. She gave him specific examples of what was said and the impact on the person concerned. Bob thanked her for being truthful and asked if she would help him overcome the issues raised. Bob's manager role-played various scenarios with him and showed him how to say 'no' positively and constructively. She gave him opportunities to test out his new approach on 'green field' customers, monitored his progress and gave him frequent and specific feedback. Six months on, she got him his promotion and pay rise. This had a hugely positive impact on both Bob and the whole of the team. Their productivity was estimated to have risen by over 50 per cent.

When giving feedback, you need to develop a mindset that views 'performance management' as something that takes place every day – not just once a year. If you can operate this way, then the annual appraisal becomes a two-way contract that sets out what you need your staff to do and what you commit to do in order to help them achieve these goals.

Asking for feedback

A common complaint amongst managers is that they do not get enough feedback on their own performance. Another is that the feedback they do get is of poor quality.

Without feedback how do you know how you are doing? Positive feedback will spur you on to do even better and developmental feedback will help you understand what areas you need to work on. When embarking on a new role this becomes even more important. A good way to get useful, timely feedback is to ask for it.

To encourage others to give you feedback, you have to make it easy for them and for them to feel good about the process (more on this below). So reward them by taking their comments seriously; be gracious about praise, explore criticism, experiment with suggestions and thank them.

Receiving feedback

This is 'pay off' time in the world of feedback. This is the point at which you learn something valuable about the impact you have on others and your organisation as a whole. Does it line up with your expectations? If so, great, if not, listen carefully and accept the feedback with good grace. Do not be defensive but do explore their reasoning. Remember, it may not be easy for the giver either, so do not make it more difficult for them; help the giver say what they really want to say. I will elaborate on this point further in the next section.

HINTS AND TIPS

Providing developmental feedback is a key management skill and one that needs to be learned. Training, reviewing both good and bad examples and on-the-job coaching will all help. Some people will inevitably find it easier than others – if it does not come naturally to you, it just means you will have to work a little harder to develop the skill.

When giving feedback, you should:

- Focus on both the positive and the negative – everyone needs encouragement and to feel valued and appreciated. In addition, if people are to progress they also need to understand their areas for improvement.

- Look at performance outcomes rather than the inner person; always separate behaviour from the person. You are entitled to comment on behaviour – indeed, as a manager, it is part of your job to encourage certain behaviours and change others – but always treat the person with respect and as an adult. Help them to see how their performance affects the people they interact with and how it contributes to the whole. For example, it is not acceptable to tell someone that they are useless and their report writing is rubbish. It is, however, both acceptable and beneficial to tell them that other people find their reports difficult to read and inconclusive and you therefore intend to send them on a report writing course so that they can improve their skills in this area.

- If people get defensive it is normally because they feel attacked as a person. If you limit your comments to aspects of their behaviour, as in the example above, they will usually work with you to solve the problem.

- Focus on the specific rather than the general – 'I liked it when you offered to help Jane with that demanding customer' rather than 'There was a very friendly atmosphere'. In that way, people can learn from it and do it again. You cannot 'do' a friendly atmosphere again, but you can help someone with a difficult customer again. If you make a general observation, follow it up with a specific example.

- Use observation rather than interpretation – i.e. what you saw them do or heard them say – rather than how you interpreted their behaviour. For example, 'You started looking through your other papers' rather than 'You weren't listening to me'.

- Use descriptions rather than judgements – describe what you saw and/or heard and how that made you (and/or others) feel. Remember, feelings are the intangible facts and deserve consideration – for example, 'When you shout in meetings, people can get really scared' rather than 'You deliberately try to frighten people'.

- Focus on questions rather than statements – questions give the recipient the responsibility of reaching their own conclusions and forces them to think about the issues and/or their behaviour. For example, 'How do you think Bob felt when you started looking through your papers?' or 'What effect do you think it has when you shout at your staff?'

- Use comparisons rather than damnation – make evaluations against agreed criteria, past performance or competitive benchmarks. Explore any discrepancies without assigning blame. Identify 'high' and 'low' points of performance and the specific behaviours that appear to contribute to, or limit, success. Make suggestions regarding possible means of improving performance. Never compare performance with that of another member of the team.

- Be prepared to deal with unexpected welfare issues such as divorce, bullying and so on. If this occurs, listen with sensitivity and, depending on the severity of the situation, seek guidance from your HR department or a peer with more experience than you in dealing with such situations.

Before concluding your discussions, check that the messages have been understood and received as you intended – watch body language (see Chapter 25 for insights on reading body language) and ask your staff member to summarise what has been agreed. Remember that this is an opportunity to build trust, respect and reciprocity – ask them what they need from you and agree how you need to provide that support and by when. Table 3.1 is a summary of helpful and unhelpful feedback.

Finally, remember that nothing contained within a formal appraisal should be a surprise to the recipient. Feedback should be a continual process – it should be regular and timely. The formal appraisal process should be an opportunity to review and summarise all that has already been said over the past appraisal period and, even more impor- tantly, it should be viewed as an opportunity to discuss future growth and learning.

Table 3.1 Helpful and unhelpful feedback

Helpful feedback	Unhelpful feedback
• is easy to understand and put into context;	• is coded or out of context;
• is specific and direct – has examples and consequences;	• is general or vague;
• matters – it is important enough to comment on;	• is unimportant or trivial;
• focuses on behaviour that can be changed;	• imposes your own values (e.g. 'that was really stupid');
• is 'owned' by you (i.e. clearly labelled as yours, what you believe, how you feel);	• makes judgements about attitudes, impact and intentions and decides for the other person what they ought to change;
• leaves choices for the recipient (e.g. 'could do' rather than 'should do');	• is based on hearsay (e.g. 'Fred thinks that you ...');
• is delivered with honesty and kindness;	• is too prescriptive – focuses on outcomes rather than process; people need to be free to do things their way;
• is timely – it needs to be given as soon as possible after the event as the effect reduces if you delay;	• results in hurt feelings, emotional barriers and defensive behaviours;
• is controlled, objective, given calmly and with sensitivity.	• can spin out of control with the potential consequences of the procedures, a refusal to sign off an initiation of grievance appraisal or an appeal.

Feedback should also always be a two-way process, so let us now turn our attention to both asking for – if it is not offered – and receiving feedback.

When asking for feedback, you should:

- Make it easy for the person concerned – keep it informal, warn them in advance, have the discussion on their territory or neutral ground and do not assume that they will reciprocate.

- Do the hard work yourself – be open, truthful and specific. Ask what they would like you to do more of or start doing and what they would like you to do less of or stop doing rather than asking them to judge you or 'rate' you.

- Ask them how you can be of most value to them, whoever they are, and use them as a sounding board.

- Explain why you are interested and why you are asking for feedback. Ask for their suggestions for improvement and actively listen to them. Explore their ideas rather than defending your position.

- Express your true reactions to what you hear – this means describing your immediate feelings.

- Act on the things you agree with, discuss the things you do not and keep an open mind - they might just have a point!

Much will depend on the openness of the culture. By encouraging honest and constructive feedback to be directed at yourself, you will help create a safe and open environment for everyone else.

When receiving feedback, you should:

- Actively listen – no interruptions and no escaping into defensive strategy building. Just concentrate on what is being said and mentally note questions or disagreements.

- Reflect back – summarise your understanding to check that you got the intended message and to show that you were listening. Their views are valid even if you disagree; perception is in the eye of the beholder.

- Explore where they are coming from – you may or may not agree with what you hear, but try to understand what is being said and why they have said it. Stay calm, show interest and probe for specific details. Seek examples in those areas that are unclear or in which disagreement exists. Paraphrase again.

- Ask for more feedback on this or any other topic. 'That's extremely helpful; are there any other areas in which this is causing a problem?'

- Express your honest reactions – this includes your feelings. 'I'm not really surprised, but I am disappointed that ...'.

- Carefully evaluate what you have heard for accuracy and potential value. Make a summary statement of where you stand now.

- Thank them – you owe them that, but nothing else. Do not allow yourself to be manipulated into acting against your better judgement or reciprocating by saying something nice (or nasty!) back.

Never 'put down' the giver because they have embarrassed you with praise. They have given you a 'gift'. Accept it graciously. Never put down a critic either – it is a cheap shot and a purely defensive response. Remember, you are always learning.

Act on what you have learned, but only if you want to. At the end of the day, the choice for how you behave is yours and yours alone. More information means more informed choices and, with judgement, better outcomes.

Experimentation with new behaviours and long-term change for the better are the ultimate rewards for both the giver and the receiver of feedback. Whether you follow it or not, never underestimate the reward power you exert by listening seriously to the giver. There is just as much in it for them as there is for you.

4 DEALING WITH POOR PERFORMANCE

WHY IS THIS IMPORTANT?

The pressure to produce and deliver more with less is probably greater today than it ever has been before, and if certain members in a team do not pull their weight, then those who do so are under even greater pressure.

Poor performers inject most of the mistakes and errors into a task, which usually has a knock-on effect down the line, resulting in re-work, fire-fighting and customer dissatisfaction. It is estimated that when re-work or fire-fighting occurs they increase the cost of an IT project by a factor of 10.

In addition, poor performers can infect an organisation like a virus, demotivating others in their wake. They get passed around from pillar to post as each manager, in turn, tries to rid themselves of the problem by passing them on to some other unsuspecting manager. As a consequence, poor performers often have a history of glowing recommendations and appraisals, because no one is likely to take on what is known to be a problem person. When successive managers fail to address the poor performance issue and duck the problem, it becomes very difficult, if not impossible, to take the person through formal disciplinary procedures when they do eventually get a manager with the courage to do so.

Dealing with poor performance is difficult, time-consuming and fraught with danger; hence it is often avoided. For many organisations, in particular the more traditional and longer-standing ones, dealing with poor performance is one of the principal 'zones of uncomfortable debate', i.e. a key issue that needs to be addressed, is holding the organisation back but is just too uncomfortable to talk about.

In virtually every organisation, people are the biggest budget item and, if performance issues are not dealt with, it will have a significant impact on the bottom line of that organisation. Successfully dealing with poor performance will also greatly enhance your reputation as a manager; with your team, your peers and your seniors.

DELVING A LITTLE DEEPER INTO THE SUBJECT

There are two key aspects that contribute towards one's performance: capability and attitude. When we talk about capability, we are considering the holistic combination of a person's knowledge, skills and experience. When we talk about attitude, we are considering their willingness to contribute, to collaborate and to learn – all of which should be done with a positive intent for the greater good.

When dealing with poor performance, it is important to distinguish between temporary glitches and long-term degradation. The former needs to be nipped in the bud swiftly and simply by following the steps you will find at the beginning of the next section.

In the case of long-term degradation in performance, it is important to understand the root causes and to work with the person to reverse the trend. The model in Figure 4.1 helps us to make sense of a situation and identify the root cause.

Figure 4.1 Performance portfolio

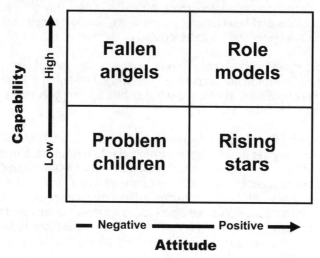

I will briefly explain the performance portfolio and in the next section give advice and guidance as to how you might deal with people in each of the four quadrants.

'Problem children' with low capability and a negative attitude

These people are your biggest challenge. They have neither the capability nor the right attitude. They could be young, insecure and just starting out; they could be approaching retirement and 'marking time'; or they may have been left in the wrong job for too long and become disillusioned. Whatever the reason, they will need coaching, counselling and motivating in order to move them to a better place.

'Rising stars' with low capability and a positive attitude

These are people with the right attitude, but without the necessary capability. They may be youngsters just starting out, members of your team who have just taken on a new role or people who have been promoted too soon. Training and development may be the answer in the case of the former. In the case of the latter, you may need to consider adjustment to their role or even changing it for a more suitable one. Either way, employees in this category need to be nurtured and protected. It is important to recognise that whenever someone takes on a new role, they will, by definition, be lacking capability so the key issue is how quickly they can adjust and get up to speed. People who find themselves on the management fast-track tend to be those who demonstrate a clear capacity for rapid adjustment to new demands and an ability to achieve a high level of competence very quickly.

'Fallen angels' with high capability and a negative attitude

These people have the capability, but the wrong attitude. You will need to uncover the reason for the negative attitude and then tackle the issue head on. They may be under-utilised and bored; they may be in the wrong job and hence unhappy; they may be distracted by a personal issue; or they may be simply just plain lazy. In the case of the latter, virtually everyone can be motivated to do something; the key is finding out what that something is (see Chapters 25 and 28 for more on motivational tools).

'Role models' with high capability and a positive attitude

These people are your top performers; the challenge here is to ensure that they remain so. In order to achieve this, they will need to be cherished and rewarded. If you let complacency set in, and just expect them to get on with it, they will either get demotivated or leave. Role models need to be stretched and challenged. Initially this will be by giving them greater exposure to decision-making, cross-functional activities and forward planning. As they grow further, you will need to find opportunities for them to leave you, but grow in the wider business. You must therefore accept that people in this role-model quadrant will, and indeed must, leave you and that your job is to make sure that, when they move on, they do so within your organisation and they do so for a more challenging job. Remember that, although you lose them, you will enhance your own reputation as a manager for being able to develop good people quickly, and as a result more 'role models' will want to come and work for you for their own career development.

You will find practical advice on how to deal with each of the four different types of performer in the next section.

HINTS AND TIPS

Before you speak to the person concerned

If there is a problem, challenge yourself to ensure that you are not part of it. Ask yourself the following questions – you will need to be brutally honest in your answers:

- Have you clearly communicated what is expected in terms of outcome, i.e. what needs to be achieved, when it needs to be achieved by and how success will be measured?

- Does the person have the appropriate skills or have they undergone the necessary training to enable them to complete the task?

- Do they have access to the information and resources they need?
- Are you adopting an appropriate leadership style in your dealings with this person?
- Have you delegated with sufficient clarity?
- Have you been there to provide support and guidance when needed?
- Have you adequately prioritised so that they understand what is important and why?
- Is this a real issue and not one of personality clash or difference in style?

If any of the above does apply, you should fix the problem first and, if appropriate, be honest about your own part in creating the issue. Once you have addressed any issues of your own making, or assured yourself that none of the above applies, you must ensure that you have the real-time evidence to support your claim of poor performance. It is not sufficient to rely on hearsay or opinion.

Dealing with short-term glitches in performance

Tackle the issue in a timely manner, i.e. shortly after it occurs. Do not wait for appraisal time – this is far, far too late. You should immediately take the following steps in this order:

- Tell them very clearly that their performance is not of an acceptable standard and why.
- Give them the opportunity to explain why their performance is not up to standard. If, for example, something dreadful had happened to a family member the previous day, you would feel very foolish if you had just criticised them for not performing at their best.
- While they are explaining the situation, shut up and actively listen to what they have to say; do not interrupt or contradict.
- Be very clear about the effect of their performance on others and in the wider context of the organisation as a whole.
- Say how you feel about the situation.
- State, explicitly, what is at stake.
- Confirm a common understanding of the issue and then agree a sequence of steps necessary to rectify the situation.
- Agree any follow-up actions that you, as their manager, need to take.
- Make sure that they have a workable plan for what they need to do and agree when and how you will check on their progress. Thank them for their input.
- Keep clear records to aid follow-up activities and support future conversations.
- Keep on top of the situation – do not expect a quick fix, but also do not let it slip off your priority list.

Dealing with long-term performance problems

If the problem persists, you will need to use a feedback and developmental approach appropriate to the person's capability and attitude. My advice for long-term issues will therefore be structured around the 'performance portfolio' depicted in Figure 4.1.

Dealing with your problem children

The first step is to find out what the problem is with your problem child. Are they a nervous starter or long-serving cynic? Have they been over-promoted or ended up a round peg in a square hole? Once you have identified the root cause, you will need to determine the most appropriate corrective action. This may include any one or a number of the following:

- Training – would the person benefit from either skill-based training or behavioural training?

- Coaching – would this person benefit from being asked some probing questions to challenge their thinking and behaviour, or some reflective questions to get them thinking about why they did what they did? You should also encourage them to examine honestly the motives that underpinned their actions. Finally, you need to help them think through the effect that their poor performance is having on others (see Chapter 28 for more on coaching and questioning techniques).

- Mentoring – are they lacking in self-confidence and in need of reassurance or affirmation from someone with greater experience?

- Motivation – could you enhance their role in any way to make it more appealing to them?

- Counselling – do they need professional help to resolve a personal issue?

- Consider a change in job role – are they in the right job? Have they been over-promoted and are they struggling with both the task and their emotions as a consequence? Are they in a role that plays to their weaknesses rather than their strengths?

- If none of the above strategies achieve the desired result, you may need to take people through formal disciplinary procedures. Ensure that you follow the formal process as laid down by your HR department, starting with an informal verbal warning and progressing, if need be, to formal written warnings.

- As a last resort, you might need to consider managing them out of the organisation or towards early retirement. Here is where you may benefit from the assistance of your HR department and outplacement organisations.

Dealing with your rising stars

The first step is to understand their potential. It is always useful to get the input from others on this one as we can often have a biased view of our own team members. Are they bright, able and quick to learn, or do they get there through tenacity and hard work?

Once you have established their potential and what interests and motivates them, you will be able to agree an appropriate developmental plan. Your prime tools will include:

- Training – this may be skill-based or behavioural training.

- Coaching – would this person benefit from being asked some probing questions to clarify their understanding of what is expected of them and how confident they feel in achieving it, some explorative questions to open their mind to new possibilities or some fresh questions to challenge their basic thinking and 'eternal truths'? (See Chapter 28 for more on coaching and questioning techniques.)

- Mentoring – would this person benefit from mirroring someone with greater experience or guidance in their judgement of situations and their consequential decision-making?

Dealing with your fallen angels

The first step is to uncover the root cause of the bad attitude. Is it because they have ended up in a role that bores them to tears? Are they unhappy, disgruntled, feeling bullied or just plain lazy? Have they been ignored, forgotten about or ended up in the wrong job? You may wish to consider:

- Coaching – would this person benefit from being asked some probing questions to invite more detail in relation to their attitude problem, some reflective questions to get them thinking about why they behave the way they do and to examine their motives, some affective questions to consider the effect their attitude is having on others or some explorative questions to open their mind to new perspectives? (See Chapter 28 for more on coaching and questioning techniques.)

- Mentoring – could the issue be one of lack of self-confidence? If so, they may be in need of affirmation or guidance from someone with greater experience than themselves.

- Counselling – do they need professional help to resolve a personal issue?

- Do they feel bullied? If so, the problem may well lie at your doorstep. Are you expecting too much or pushing too hard? Do not assume that everyone is ambitious, many people are happy to maintain a certain level.

- Job enrichment – could you enhance or supplement their role to make it more fulfilling/appealing?

- Consider a change in job role – do they need greater responsibility or a new challenge?

- If none of the above strategies achieve the desired result, you may need to take people through formal disciplinary procedures. Ensure that you follow the formal process as laid down by your HR department, starting with an informal verbal warning and progressing, if need be, to formal written warnings.

As a last resort, you might need to consider managing them out of the organisation or towards early retirement. Here is where you may benefit from the assistance of your HR department and outplacement organisations.

Ensuring your role models remain just that

The final quadrant of the model deals with people you have classified as role models. You would not expect to have performance issues with these people, but that does not mean that you can afford to ignore them. Your focus should be on maintaining and sustaining actions and providing intellectual and professional challenge.

Such valuable members of your team will need to be cherished, nurtured and rewarded; if you do not, they will either leave or become fallen angels. Focus on the following actions:

- Provide opportunities for personal development and preparing them for the next step up.

- Give them frequent and positive feedback – ensure that they know that they are doing a good job and that they know how much you value and appreciate them.

- Coach them – specifically in areas where they will need to exercise judgement and decision-making. Stretch them and encourage them to aim for higher goals. Challenge them to think the unthinkable and to generate new insights (see Chapter 28 for more on coaching and questioning techniques).

- Reward their achievements and celebrate their successes.

- Give them opportunities to represent you in discussions with other departments/ businesses.

- Help them to develop their circle of influence and to develop wider knowledge of the business and its operating environment (see Chapter 21 for advice on networking).

- Involve them in discussions about strategic direction and planning the development of junior colleagues.

- Identify opportunities for them to act as coaches for junior colleagues.

- Think about possible ways to enhance their job to increase their job satisfaction.

Any discussions about performance issues will be emotionally charged. Therefore, it is imperative that you remember the importance of tone, body language and facial expression (see Chapter 25 for insights on reading body language). Make use of silence to help both of you think about what you really want to say and to ensure that there is space for reflection and active listening. It is important at all times that you engage in a genuine two-way conversation rather than letting your discussions deteriorate into a one-way monologue.

Get to know your staff; understand both their hearts and their minds. Ensure that the dialogue is ongoing. Use active questioning to establish what excites and what frustrates them. Actively listen to the nuances and subtext to get beneath the surface. Develop a strong interest in motivational psychology (see Further Reading for book suggestions). Be prepared to invest time and effort; dealing with poor performance and developing people is time-consuming, but this is your prime purpose as a manager and leader of people. Your reward will be motivated, happy, energised and loyal staff. You will also enhance your reputation as a manager of people.

5   DEVELOPING TEAMS

WHY IS THIS IMPORTANT?

The term 'team' is much overused and in most organisational settings is synonymous with a bunch of people who happen to work for someone by virtue of their position in the organisational hierarchy. Yet, a team has the capacity to be far more than just a bunch of people – individuals are not perfect, but teams can be.

Your job as a manager is to harness the capabilities of your 'bunch of people' and give them both a sense of direction and a modicum of freedom so that they become a mutually supportive collective that takes a pride in achieving significant and measureable outcomes.

Leading a team is not just a matter of saying and doing the right things – how you behave and the values that you live by speak more eloquently and carry more weight than you may think. Deeds speak louder than words, and consistency, transparency and fairness will help to build trust and engender loyalty.

DELVING A LITTLE DEEPER INTO THE SUBJECT

Teamwork is not a matter of luck. Real teams tend to have a number of common features and a characteristic culture. These are as follows:

- they are made up of a small number of people – somewhere between four and eight;
- they have complementary skills;
- the leadership may rotate depending on the task;
- they are engaged in the production of a collective work product;
- they are united in a shared purpose;
- all members work with positive intentions towards the collective good;
- everyone understands each other, i.e. their role, responsibilities and personalities.

Take, for example, a surgical team: it would typically comprise an anaesthetist, one or two surgeons and two or three nurses. They all have very different, but very necessary, skill-sets. In the beginning the anaesthetist is in charge, then the leadership passes on to the surgeon and finally to the scrub nurse. They are all focused on the patient with the aim of making him or her better. They are all working with positive intentions – to save or extend a life or improve its quality. They understand and anticipate each other's moves and needs. There is humour and light-hearted banter.

Now let us consider this list in greater detail:

- **A small number of people** – too few and there is insufficient diversity of skills, talents, experience, personality type and so on. Too many and discussions either get protracted and boredom sets in or, alternatively, people get left out and subsequently disengage.

- **Complementary skills** – as mentioned above: 'Individuals aren't perfect, but teams can be'. We all have strengths and weaknesses, and no one is good at everything. However, if a team has a good mix of talents and capabilities, it can cover all the bases.

- **Rotating leadership** – depending on the stage of the project or task, leadership is given to the best person for the job and as the requirement changes, leadership shifts as appropriate. For example, if the team is in data-gathering mode, leadership should sit with someone who is good with the details, or when in brainstorming mode, the lead should be with your ideas person.

- **Collective work product** – the team is focused on a specific outcome or course of action, which means that they are all aligned in what is to be achieved and clear as to what the final outcome should be.

- **A shared purpose** – a top-down edict seldom creates a shared purpose. A shared purpose that inspires and ignites action comes from the team itself; from curiosity, questioning and challenging each other to achieve something special.

- **Positive intentions towards the collective good** – all team members have a willingness to truly cooperate and to give freely of their own personal resources to help each other. In addition there is preparedness to compromise on individual interests in order to achieve the best overall result.

Indeed, the car manufacturer, Ferrari, put their racing success, for a record six consecutive years between 1999 and 2004, down to teamwork. They created an ethos within the company such that all the critical components were developed together to optimise the whole package – the Ferrari itself. 'It's not an engine, it's not an aero-package, it's not a chassis, it's a Ferrari' (Jenkins et al. 2005).

All the departmental heads shared a common vision and they were all prepared to compromise on their individual departmental interests in order to get the best overall result.

- **Everyone understands each other** – real teams have a sense of camaraderie and engage in friendly banter. Team members display a sense of humour and there is laughter in the office; they talk and listen in roughly equal measures; they listen respectfully and without interrupting; there is empathy when teammates are in trouble and sensitivity to the views and feelings of each other.

29

HINTS AND TIPS

You can teach people how to communicate, how to be interesting and engaging, how to be sensitive to the needs of others and such like. However, it is very, very difficult to teach someone to be a team player. Team players are people with the natural desire to be helpful and cooperative, people who will not hog the limelight but who will help their colleagues shine. These characteristics tend to be innate; something you either do or do not have. Highly competitive people are seldom team players as they are always looking to upstage or outsmart their team mates. Equally, highly independent people seldom make good team players either as they do not look to involve or include and do not necessarily value the input of others.

So, ideally, you would want to start with the right raw material. Indeed, this was the strategy of the car manufacturer, Renault, and of the other top performing F1 racing teams during the early part of this century. Their focus was on teamwork, sharing ideas and learning from the past. In order to achieve this they were very clear about the kind of engineers they needed to recruit. 'We look for people who think laterally, who never accept that something is impossible and who are prepared to work hard. They should be individualistic in their thinking, but team players in their actions' (Jenkins et al. 2005).

While you are unlikely to have a team full of team players there are a number of things that you can do to encourage teamwork. Consider the seating and physical layout of your office space. Is it conducive to teamwork? Are people facing each other or facing the walls? Are there high screens blocking one's view of others? Are people able and allowed to personalise their space?

Initiate something like a common coffee break where all team members have the opportunity to interact informally. Having a drink after work or going for an evening out can also be good from a team-bonding perspective, though may not be possible because of outside commitments or cultural or religious sensitivities. You would not want to exclude any team member, so you will need to make a judgement as to what would work best for your particular team.

Study your team members as individuals; some may be more naturally inclusive than others, some may be more talkative and outspoken, some may be bossier than others and some may be more open in their personal disclosure. You may need to encourage some of your team to listen more, not to interrupt others and draw the quieter ones out. Equally, you may need to encourage other members of your team to make better eye contact and speak out. For example, in a meeting simply say 'George, I would value your thoughts on this one' or 'Fred, do you have anything to add?'. You can also give them informal feedback outside the meeting as to how you would like them to behave, and how you intend to help them overcome their internal barriers and motivate them to give it a go (see Chapter 3 for more on giving feedback). Your aim is to ensure everyone is engaged and contributing without monopolising.

If your team is new, it may be helpful to kick-start the team-bonding process with a team-building event. Psychometric instruments, such as the Myers Briggs Type Indicator®, can be very helpful in helping team members understand each other's personality type, preferred communication style and as an aid to valuing and appreciating difference. If you do embark on such an initiative you will need to engage the services of a professional – if not done properly it may do more harm than good.

Role model the behaviour you want to encourage – set personal examples. If you wish to encourage more face-to-face communication, that is what you must exhibit yourself. If you wish to encourage your team to work together to resolve problems, then again that is the behaviour you need to adopt yourself. The following mini case is a good illustration of such behaviour.

Sarah was a well-liked member of the team, but struggled in her role as a database administrator. It wasn't for want of trying, she just could not find solutions to problems she had never come across. The basic problems were OK, but the complicated stuff was just beyond her capability.

Her team members were torn between frustration and annoyance because she was not pulling her weight and their wish to support and cover for her because they liked her as a person. The consequence was an underperforming team.

Her manager took the situation in hand with the help of her team members. He first spoke to them without her being there and asked for their advice and suggestions in the spirit of achieving a win–win outcome. Once he had a potential solution he then put it to Sarah to see if it appealed to her.

In essence he 'sculpted' her job to make it more suitable to her abilities, but also agreeable to the rest of her team in terms of contribution. The solution was that she would take on full responsibility for the more routine aspects of the job and leave her teammates to deal with the more complex issues. In return she would be the official, permanent out-of-hours contact with a fistful of phone numbers to call if she needed help. Her team were happy because they had rid themselves of the boring tasks and also no longer had to compromise their social lives to be 'on call'. She was happy because she suddenly felt valued and respected by her team and her boss, she felt she was contributing and she really did not mind being permanently 'on call' – indeed, it made her feel important. As a consequence, re-work was a thing of the past, mistakes were virtually eliminated and productivity almost doubled.

So what can you do if you get landed or stuck with individuals who are not team players? If it is because they are highly independent you may be able to win them over by demonstrating the benefits of working together and showcasing lots of inclusive behaviour towards them, from consulting them on matters to asking for their ideas/options and inviting them to meetings and coffee gatherings.

The highly competitive ones are more difficult; with a bit of luck they may follow the herd and get onside. If they do not, your fall-back strategy is to neutralise their behaviour so that they do not infect the rest of your team with negative vibes. You may try negotiating their agreement by offering incentives, coercing them by threat of negative consequence, isolating them with specific duties or, if all else fails, remove them from the team.

If you have the luxury of recruiting into your team always look to bring in team players – make this your number one criteria.

Certain management practices, ones that you are unlikely to have the power to change, work against the spirit of teamwork. Rewarding individual rather than team behaviour is one of these. Stack ranking, whereby managers across a company are required to rank all of their employees on a bell curve, is another as only a small percentage of employees, typically about 10 per cent, can be designated as top performers. Meanwhile, a similar number must be labelled as low performers and are often fired or pushed out. This practice is normally only adopted by large companies and is now far more common in the States than in the UK within the corporate world. However, it is still prevalent in the UK in the public sector and, although people might not get fired, it will affect their pay rises and promotion prospects.

This type of cultural practice will discourage teamwork as it sets employees against each other, driving them to having to compete to keep their jobs, for the biggest bonus, for pay rises, for training opportunities and so on. All you can do in such situations is to be totally honest, transparent and fair. Your staff will understand your dilemma and respect your integrity.

True teamwork is very hard to attain, but this should not deter you from trying. If you can get 80 per cent of the way there, you will have done very well and achieved more than most.

REFERENCE

Jenkins, M., Pasternak, K. and West, R. (2005) *Performance at the limit: Business lessons from Formula 1 motor racing*. Cambridge: Cambridge University Press.

6   CHANGE LEADERSHIP

WHY IS THIS IMPORTANT?

As Heraclitus stated in 500BC, 'There is nothing permanent except change'. When I first started my career in IT back in the early 80s, the conventional wisdom was that there would be periods of change followed by periods of stability. In today's world of the digital era, change is no longer periodic; it is continuous and increasing at an ever-frantic pace. Every manager and leader within an organisation, from the most junior to the most senior, will be required to do their bit.

For many people, the prospect of organisational change can trigger a strong sense of unease. They may be anxious about losing things they hold dear and nervous about being asked to do things they may not want to do. As a manager, your job is to guide your team through these turbulent times. Research at the Cranfield School of Management has found that less than 10 per cent of change initiatives effectively formulated are effectively executed on account of poor change leadership.

So why is it so difficult to execute change? The answer is because it involves people. People do not always behave rationally and logically and often their behaviour is unpredictable. How many times have you attended meetings where various people have agreed to do something and subsequent to that meeting things have just not happened? The reason is that getting people to 'buy-in' intellectually to a course of action is easy, but getting them to buy-in emotionally is a lot more difficult. Without emotional as well as intellectual buy-in, change does not take place. There is always an excuse – I was too busy, the timing was wrong, it was too difficult, I will start tomorrow, etc. – but tomorrow never comes and complacency sets in. According to the change guru, Kotter, complacency, or the lack of urgency, is the biggest barrier to change. He has dubbed it the 'modern virus' and also warns 'A sense of urgency is not to be confused with frantic activity focused on meeting upon meeting, fire-fighting, back protecting, dealing with the trivial or unimportant' (Kotter, 2008).

DELVING A LITTLE DEEPER INTO THE SUBJECT

Most managers appreciate that change is a process, but most of the models used to guide managers through the process view change as something that you do to other people or systems. The reality is that, where human behaviour is concerned, change can only come from the inside; individuals must come to the decision to change for themselves, and for each person the trigger for that change will be different. You cannot force someone to change; they have got to want to change.

When faced with change, a very few people will find it exciting and exhilarating, and a similarly small proportion will even try to actively undermine or aggressively oppose it. In general, the normal reaction to change is ambivalence. Ambivalence does not mean 'I don't care'; rather, it means 'I will reserve judgement until I understand more about the proposed change or how the proposed change will affect me personally'. When change is afoot, people are often subconsciously caught in a conflict of opposed attitudes and emotions that results in competing commitments – intellectually I appreciate that the organisation needs to move forward, but personally I am concerned about the corresponding impact it might have on my role, who I report to, my physical position in the office and so on.

These competing commitments *en masse* will undermine morale and performance and could ultimately paralyse any change initiative.

People usually react to change or the threat of change at an emotional level. Much of the thought about human change comes from working with people undergoing profound change such as coping with bereavement, terminal illness or substance abuse and dependency. These ideas are then picked up, generalised and reshaped to fit the world of organisational behaviour.

The most widely known model comes from pioneering work carried out by Elizabeth Kübler-Ross and published in her book *On Death and Dying* (1969). In this she identifies five stages of transition for people facing death, namely: denial, anger, bargaining, depression and, finally, acceptance. The model was quickly appropriated by organisational psychologists, subsequently expanded and is often now termed the change curve, or the change roller coaster. A typical representation of the roller coaster is shown in Figure 6.1.

Figure 6.1 Behaviour through the change curve

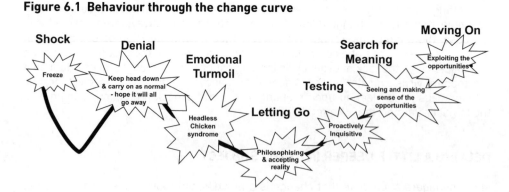

Current thinking indicates that, in order for people to find the motivation to change, they need help to confront their competing concerns and commitments. A manager's role is not to *talk at* their people about change, but rather to *engage* their people openly in 'change talk' in such a way as to allow them to explore their own competing concerns and commitments and, through this understanding, find a route to their own motivation to change.

HINTS AND TIPS

As a manager it is your job to help your organisation develop and succeed. This will inevitably involve supporting and driving change initiatives. Part of your role will be to prepare your team for change and encourage your team to embrace it. The following 10-point checklist will aid you on this mission:

1. **Effective communication** – open and honest communication about the changing world and people's places in it will reduce the shock that people tend to experience at the start of the change curve. Your team will need to understand the need for, and logic of, the change. This needs to be communicated effectively and in the language of the receiver. You will find how to do this in Chapter 8.

2. **Bring the truth into the room** – get resistance out in the open and listen to people's issues and concerns no matter how daft or trivial they sound. Ask the difficult and forbidden questions; for example, 'why do we continue to tolerate the email culture that has developed within this organisation' or 'why do we continue to put up with X's behaviour just because he is a pal of the CEO'. Uncomfortable conversations are liberating and articulating fears makes them less powerful. Remember, many issues that are raised are really personal issues just dressed up to look like business issues.

3. **Remove excuses** – how many times have you heard excuses or even made them yourself: 'I was too busy ...'; 'the timing wasn't right ...'; 'I'll do it tomorrow'. When people do not really want to do something, because it is difficult, awkward or time-consuming, they are all very good at finding reasons to put it off. So get rid of the trivial and the unimportant, or at least place them at the bottom of your agenda to provide the time and the energy. See Chapter 24 for advice on time management.

4. **Utilise peer pressure** – inevitably some members of your team will be more positive than the rest. Cultivate the more positive ones and use them as allies and advocates. Once you have a critical mass of supporters you will find that most of the rest will follow the herd and get onside.

5. **Involve, support and train people** – actively listen to those affected and be prepared to use their ideas and suggestions. Give them emotional support; sometimes a shoulder to cry on and a little time to adjust is all they need in order to come to terms with the change. Train people in new skills and behaviours, but only when the time is right. This needs to be just before you require them to use the new skills/behaviours and only once they have passed the 'letting go' stage of the change curve. There is little point in training people when they are not in a receptive frame of mind – it is akin to throwing money down the drain. When your people are trying out new skills and behaviours, build their confidence by forgiving early mistakes, making affirming statements and giving them praise and encouragement.

6. **Deal with the resisters** – most people will respond to the above methods, but for those who do not you may need to use less positive methods. You could try negotiating their agreement by offering incentives or coercing them by threat of negative consequence. For example, 'if you do X you will get a bonus or a favoured seat by the window' or, alternatively, 'if you do not do Y you will be the subject of formal disciplinary procedures'. If all else fails, manipulation, co-option or removal from the team may be your only option, but these tactics should only be used as a last resort. When using such strategies it is important to ensure that you operate 'fair process' throughout and that you send a consistent message. The theory behind fair process is that people will buy into an outcome, even if it is less than ideal for them, as long as they agree with the process that led to that outcome and perceive it to be fair.

7. **Get some help** – read books on change management, talk to peers and colleagues about their experiences and find out what has helped and what has not helped them. Learn from past experiences. The greatest learning often comes from negative experiences, so discuss them openly, but do not apportion blame or dwell on them, just ensure that you do not repeat past mistakes.

8. **Focus on the quick and easy** – all journeys begin with small steps. A long list of activities can be overwhelming and a sense of being overwhelmed is the surest way to paralyse action. Be opportunistic; pick three or four quick wins and start implementing them now. This will create the momentum, energy and confidence to take on something bigger. When you do tackle something bigger, do not spend meeting upon meeting discussing and debating. When anticipating the future there are no right answers, only choices. So make a choice and see where it takes you. If it takes you closer to where you want to go, then do more of the same; if not, then try something else. If you do something, you always move forward. If you do not, you always stand still.

9. **Engage both hearts and minds** – if you only engage the mind the best you can hope for is compliance. In order to achieve active cooperation, total commitment and ultimately championship you also need to engage the heart. In order to achieve this you yourself will need to be passionate about the change, create excitement, alleviate any fears and arouse determination to take action. Ensure that each member of your team is totally clear about the role they need to play in the change, what they need to do and how they should go about doing it. It is also crucial that each member of your team sees the 'what's in it for them'; having something positive to look forward to will galvanise action and help make the change stick.

10. **Celebrate your success** – research has demonstrated that teams and organisations that focus on, and celebrate, success are more successful than those which do not. Success becomes ingrained in the culture and people naturally look for it, focus on it and expect it. Look for opportunities to praise people genuinely: 'I liked the way you handled that meeting/difficult customer', 'I thought your conclusions in the XYZ report were spot on' and so on. Share, and encourage others to share, success stories and celebrate successful projects and implementations. Celebrate the small wins as much as the big wins. If you look for and celebrate success you will see more of it. It works for Olympic athletes, for children and for us!

The advice above assumes that you, the manager, agree with the change. But what do you do if you do not, if you genuinely believe it is the wrong thing for your organisation? Your choices are to:

- Accept it has to happen, in which case you have two further choices. You can toe the company line and tell your team it needs to happen; however, this would be a lie and is liable to destroy trust. Alternatively you can be honest and tell them that you do not believe it is the right thing to do, but you have no choice. Then you engage them in finding a solution that fulfils the organisational requirement, but with minimum pain to your team.

- Move to a different organisation, one that is a better cultural fit for you and where you do agree with senior management change initiatives.

- Challenge the change and help your boss and senior management realise that there is a better way. You will find out how to do this in Chapters 13 and 22.

REFERENCES

Kotter, J.P. (2008) *A sense of urgency*. Boston, MA: Harvard Business Press.

Kübler-Ross, E. (1969) *On death and dying*. New York: The Macmillan Company.

7 THINKING STRATEGICALLY

WHY IS THIS IMPORTANT?

Surveys show that strategic thinking is one of the top three capabilities that is valued and looked for in business leaders.

Most management competency frameworks include strategic thinking as a key skill. If you can demonstrate your capability in this area you are highly likely to be viewed as someone with 'leadership potential'.

Organisations cannot survive by just aimlessly repeating what they did last year or even last month. Organisations need to be able to respond to changing circumstances, to take advantage of emerging trends and constantly find new ways of delighting their customers with new levels of service and products that were previously unimaginable. In today's world nothing is having a greater impact on the way things work and on the products and services organisations can offer than technological advancements and the possibilities that they create.

To this end, a fundamental capability for all managers is the ability to initiate and bring about change. But an organisation needs its change initiatives to be aligned towards a common purpose – that purpose is articulated in the business strategy and every manager needs to be able to internalise that strategy to the extent where it provides a guiding framework for their decision-making.

DELVING A LITTLE DEEPER INTO THE SUBJECT

Strategic thinkers are people who can think holistically and see beyond the limits of the current issue or the obvious. They take a broad perspective on how a proposed course of action can contribute to the achievement of the long-term goals of an organisation as a whole as well as resolving the immediate local problem.

When you are busy and stressed and faced with a critical problem, it can be difficult to find either the time or the perspective to see beyond the bounds of the immediate. Always try to broaden your perspective and maintain your focus on the long-term objectives. When you fix things with an eye to the long-term effects or consequences, they tend to stay fixed. On the other hand, if you make your decisions based solely on the effects in the here and now, the problems have a nasty habit of coming back to bite you.

The more managers within an organisation behave in this manner, the greater the decision-making alignment of that organisation and the more effective it becomes.

So what is strategic thinking and how is it different from the rest of the thinking we do? An important skill of strategic thought is the ability to take a different view of a situation. But not just any different view – what you need is a view that allows you clear sight of your objective – where you are trying to get to – while at the same time letting you see the terrain that stands between you and your objective.

A key capability is therefore to be alert to the emergence of new trends and to grasp these possibilities intelligently and opportunistically for the overall benefit of your organisations as a whole. See Chapter 16 for advice on how to harness the potential of IT.

HINTS AND TIPS

In order to think strategically you need to think beyond the immediate and the obvious. Take a holistic view of your organisation and consider how the various parts of the organisation are interconnected. Focus on what is possible instead of how situations have been handled in the past.

Begin with the end in mind, i.e. focus on the outcome you wish to achieve, the need to be fulfilled or problem to be solved. This is sometimes referred to as 'outcome-focused thinking'.

Next consider what needs to be in place to make this outcome more likely to come about in the future. This is sometimes referred to as 'backward-pass thinking'.

Finally you need to adopt a mindset of intelligent opportunism, be alert to emerging trends and good opportunities and take advantage of them.

Consider the three examples of strategic thinking in the following case study.

A venture capital company launched a project to replace its existing worldwide infrastructure. Primarily, the project's aim was to enable employees to access their systems from any remote location. There were many investment consultants who had to remain mobile in order to fulfil their functions effectively. They were going to be able to access their systems 'any time, any place, anywhere'. The initial plan envisioned by the IT director was to provide a new system that would be much bigger and better than anything they had already, involving better data access and the biggest and best desktop equipment. It was going to be a 'Rolls Royce' solution to a real business need.

A relatively junior team leader involved in the project foresaw a potential issue with this plan, one of financial viability. He came up with an alternative idea that would be significantly cheaper. This new idea involved a different technical direction utilising, as it was then, a piece of leading edge technology known as Citrix. Citrix technology would enable the use of much cheaper desktop equipment and also provided a future proof environment, while fulfilling the 'any time, any place, anywhere' requirement at the heart of the vision.

This idea took the project in a new direction and one that ultimately won IT the admiration of its business leaders and an award for their technical design and innovative use of technology.

A manufacturing company was struggling to retain its most senior and valuable technical staff. They were rapidly becoming dependant on very expensive contract staff to fulfil critical roles. The problem was that a technician hit a glass ceiling at a certain grade unless they wanted to go into management.

A development manager proposed a way forward: to introduce a new grade, one of 'consultant technician', with a higher salary limit than middle management. She used the analogy of a hospital where the consultants treating medical conditions would have a higher status and a higher salary than many of the 'non clinical' managers 'managing' them.

Once adopted this initiative saved the company tens of thousands on its salary bill. The company also benefited from improved staff moral and safeguarded itself from losing key resources.

A Luxembourg-based bank offered investment products to high-net-worth individuals. The minimum investment was one million euros. In the beginning customers would start receiving interest on their investment the day following its deposit. However, after a few errors were made, various process and procedures were added to ensure that mistakes were not made in the future. One of the consequences of these modifications was that customers did not now receive interest on their investment until seven days after its deposit. This led to some very unhappy customers and an unknown but probable loss of business.

The risk of something going horribly wrong was low, but, if it did, the consequential financial loss would be high. The IT manager on site, looking after a team of five people, went to talk to some of the bank's competitors to ask them how they handled the situation. During her discussions with peers in other organisations an idea was born as to an alternative way of handling the issue.

The final outcome was that the bank took out an insurance policy to mitigate the risk of a mistake. It was therefore able to streamline its processes. The processing time reduced to two days and the bank benefited from happy customers and reduced administration costs. The cost of the insurance policy was far lower than the cost of the enhanced administrative processes that it replaced.

These three examples demonstrate the core skills of strategic thinking; considering the big picture, looking at the organisation as a whole, focusing on the root cause of the problem rather than merely addressing the symptoms, taking a long-term view, focusing on the outcome to be achieved and finding a way to achieve it. The people concerned strived to stretch their imagination and skill-sets to either maximise the use of resources or add value to their organisations and take them to the level of the extraordinary.

In order to get you thinking at the right level, try writing down the strategic direction of your organisation in one simple, easy-to-understand sentence. Now, within the context of that strategic direction, write down your purpose, again in one simple, easy-to-understand sentence. Finally, think of three initiatives that would make a difference to your organisation for the better. These may be only small initiatives, but they are all that is needed at this stage. This is strategic thinking.

To provide food for thought, and to help you contribute on a grander scale, take out a subscription to a magazine such as *New Scientist* or *Harvard Business Review*.

Consider your calendar over the last three months. How much of your time have you spent on tactical day-to-day management issues, and how much of your time have you spent setting future direction and motivating your team? Are you happy with this balance or does it need to change?

You will know that you have succeeded in thinking strategically when:

- You are leading the way rather than following or copying anyone else.
- You have provided direction and inspiration rather than prescription and rigidity.
- The people around you are excited by possibilities and choices.
- There is a positive atmosphere and your team feel liberated rather than constrained.
- Things are starting to happen and change for the better.
- You have time in your diary to be proactive and think about and plan for the future.

PART 2
SKILLS THAT YOU HAVE ALWAYS NEEDED
BUT ARE NOW MORE CRITICAL

8 EFFECTIVE COMMUNICATION

WHY IS THIS IMPORTANT?

Effective communication is essential; it is the lifeblood of any organisation. However, in the words of George Bernard Shaw: 'The biggest problem with communication is the illusion that it has been accomplished.'

When you become a manager your ability to communicate effectively takes on a new level of importance. You cease to become a 'doer' and you start to become a coordinator, a coach, a mentor, a motivator, a facilitator, a director, an informer and an influencer. All these new roles require good communication skills.

Without effective communication, silos develop. At best departments find themselves working in isolation and at worst they are in competition; the whole thing becomes disjointed and productivity suffers.

On an individual basis, poor communication leads to misunderstanding, wasted effort and ultimately distrust. People become demotivated because they do not see the results of their efforts, do not know what is expected of them or do not understand their purpose within the greater context of the organisation as a whole. They start to focus their energies towards speculating about the potential motives that may underpin the message rather than the content of the message and what they are required to do now.

Often, when we are the one doing the communicating and others do not seem to get our meaning, we tend to blame them and simply repeat the same messages only louder – leaving both parties feeling resentful and frustrated.

The results of poor communication within an organisation can be catastrophic. It will lead to errors, wasted effort, customer dissatisfaction, re-work and fire-fighting. IT departments are renowned for their inability to communicate effectively with the rest of the business; it is estimated that re-work and fire-fighting increase the costs of an IT project by a factor of 10.

DELVING A LITTLE DEEPER INTO THE SUBJECT

Communication does not have a 'one-size-fits-all approach'. What works for one person will not necessarily work for another. In order to communicate effectively you will need to tailor your communications to the receiver and deliver the message in their preferred 'language'. So how do you establish what someone's preferred language is?

The following technique, based on Carl Jung's theory of psychological type, helps to put some science behind the objective. His theory describes two prime dimensions that are of fundamental importance in relation to communication style. The two dimensions are:

- **Level of detail** – some people like all the facts and lots of detail while others just want the big picture or 'headline'.

- **Basis for decision-making** – some people base their decision-making on objective logic; others base their decision-making on subjective values and the impact of their decisions on the person or people concerned.

These two dimensions are used to generate the matrix in Figure 8.1 that describes the four resulting 'types' of people, each with their own fundamentally different communication style and needs.

Figure 8.1 Communication needs

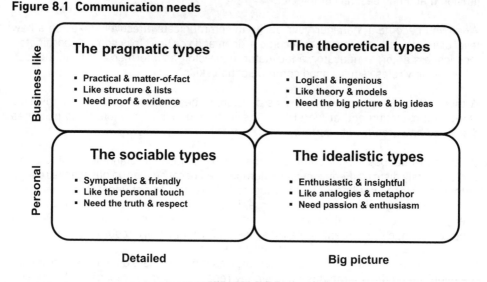

- **The pragmatic types** like facts and are cautious not to go beyond the facts. They rely upon their five senses to guide them and favour literal interpretation of data. They make decisions through logical analysis of data and other empirical evidence, evaluating the pros and cons of all the possible options. Their objective is to reach fair, reasoned and rational conclusions.

- **The theoretical types** like ideas, theories and concepts. They read between the lines and value the interpretation of such insights. They need to have an answer to the big 'Why?' question. They rely upon gut instinct and sixth sense in their decision-making, intuitively knowing the answer or way forward. They pursue their chosen course of action with confidence and certainty. Their objective is to make sense of the world by making connections and building mental models. They seek to find ways of helping others to see and to bring clarity from disorder.

- **The idealistic types** like the figurative and the symbolic. They are ingenious and creative and are interested in the complexities of communication, the patterns underlying immediate facts and theoretical relationships. Their insights are focused on human relationships and future possibilities. Their objective is to make the world a better place, whatever 'better' constitutes in their view of the world.

- **The sociable types** are interested in facts, but facts about people rather than facts about things. They are grounded in the present reality and focus their efforts on practical benefits for individuals. They value collegiality and harmony, are approving and uncritical and exercise sympathy and sentiment in their decision-making. Values and emotions determine what is right and form the basis of their decision-making. They will also take into account the impact of their decisions on the people concerned. Their objective is to make the world a nicer place.

If you can learn to tailor your communication and speak the language of the recipient, you are far more likely to engage them and ensure your message is received as you intended.

HINTS AND TIPS

For communication to be effective you need to tick a number of boxes. You will need to:

- consider your style of communication;
- promote an open dialogue;
- get the timing right;
- use an appropriate place;
- consider the medium of your communication;
- ensure that you are clear in your own mind as to the purpose of your communication.

Take into account both the message you wish to convey and the person or people you need to convey it to. Choose wisely and appropriately. Be prepared to exercise both patience and pragmatism and remember that, when you are communicating with groups of people, you may need to use more than one style and/or method.

The appropriate style

Use the theory described in the previous section to tailor your communication to the preferred language of the receiver – treat people how they would wish to be treated rather than how you would wish to be treated.

This means you need to listen to the way people communicate and watch how they respond towards the communication attempts of others. The following guidelines will help you to make a 'best guess' as to someone's type:

The pragmatic types will:

- Be interested in facts, use precise language and learn from experience.
- Give you lots of information and lists longer than three items.
- Make decisions based on the facts utilising impersonal and logical analysis from cause to effect, from premise to conclusion.
- Use a step-by-step sequential approach to describe a situation, starting at the beginning and working through to the end.
- Use the words 'thinking' or 'thought' rather than 'feeling' or 'felt'.

The theoretical types will:

- Be interested in possibilities, theoretical relationships and abstract concepts.
- Give impressions rather than details and short lists no longer than three items.
- Be quick in their decision-making, using intuition coupled with impersonal objectivity; they are confident individuals with a strong sense of self-worth.
- Use analogies and anecdotes to illustrate a situation and leave you with impressions rather than details.
- Use the words 'thinking' or 'thought' rather than 'feeling' or 'felt'.

The idealistic types will:

- Be interested in possibilities, symbolic meanings, things that have never happened but might be made to happen, or truths that are not yet known but might be.
- Give you impressions rather than detail and lists no longer than three items.
- Make decisions based on their own personal values and the impact of those decisions on others; their aim will be to make the world a better place, whatever 'better' is in their book.
- Use analogies and anecdotes to illustrate a situation and leave you with impressions rather than details.
- Use the words 'feeling' or 'felt' rather than 'thinking' or 'thought'.

The sociable types will:

- Be interested in facts, but facts about real people and true stories about what has helped these real people.
- Give information and stories about real people and their experiences and give you lists longer than three items.
- Make decisions based on facts with personal warmth, weighing how much things matter to them and to others.
- Use the words 'feeling' or 'felt' rather than 'thinking' or 'thought'.

Once you have made a 'best guess' as to someone's type, the next step is to test it.

A pragmatic person will need honesty and clarity, and specific and relevant facts. They will appreciate a pragmatic, common-sense approach. The following are tools that will help when communicating with them:

- Use a sequential, step-by-step approach when explaining a situation or event.
- Give specifics: the what, why, who, when and a clear plan of action.
- If possible, offer proof and evidence that it has worked for others.
- Focus on the tried and tested rather than the novel or the unusual.
- Make sure all the numbers add up.
- Be accurate and precise and give *all* but *only* relevant information in support of your case.
- Keep it business-like; do not get too personal or over-evangelical.
- Focus on the hard facts rather than the effect on the people and their feelings about it; conclude with the impact on the 'bottom line'.

A theoretical person will want you to be business-like, concise, to the point and focus on the big picture. They will need you to answer the big question 'Why?'. Start with your idea, proposal or conclusion, remove most of the detail and back it up with a few key high-level facts. The following are tools that will help when communicating with them:

- Keep lists short as theoretical types tend to think in threes – three key facts, three reasons why and so on.
- Focus on models and theories rather than pictures and images.
- Focus on results and objectives rather than on the effect on people and their feelings about it.
- Allow them to have an input – this will allow them to make whatever you are proposing their idea.
- Be direct and to the point, do not hesitate or waffle, and radiate confidence.

An idealistic person will want unique treatment, and for you to listen carefully and show an interest in their ideas. Try to inject passion and humour into your conversation, demonstrate that you truly believe in what you are saying and make it sound exciting. The following are things that will help when communicating with them:

- Focus on the idea or concept, not the detail as to how you arrived at it.
- Use imagery and metaphor rather than fact or theory to impart your message.
- Ask them for their input.
- Talk about the 'greater good', about 'making a difference' to humanity at large rather than individual people; remember, in the mind of the idealistic type individuals are expendable for the good of the masses.

A sociable person will want to build a personal connection with you. They will want you to demonstrate empathy and practicality, to tell the truth, the whole truth and nothing but the truth. The following are tools that will help when communicating with them:

- Give facts and details, but facts and details about real people.
- Avoid generalisations or impersonal language such as 'downsizing' or 'rightsizing'; talk instead about the effects on Fred, Joe and Harry.
- Demonstrate caring and empathy towards individual people.
- Ask open questions and probe gently; actively listen and encourage them to do most of the talking; do not patronise them or talk at them.
- Avoid big intuitive leaps or off-the-wall ideas; focus on the practical realities of today.

Always remember that this is only a guess, so be prepared to re-evaluate. If people respond positively to your communication style, carry on; however, if they appear bored, disinterested or get frustrated, try an alternative approach. Also bear in mind that these are broad generalisations and not everyone will fit neatly into one of the four categories. The most important things to remember are to be sensitive to the needs of others and to be flexible in your communication style and approach.

Promote an open dialogue

Dialogue is so much more than just a conversation. When you are in dialogue with someone you are engaged in a mutual search for purpose and insight rather than trying to get your point across. It requires you to let go of your ego and opinions and listen without judging. When you participate in effective dialogue, you will:

- establish common ground;
- explore and challenge previously unexamined or unstated assumptions;
- explore new ideas and perspectives;
- learn to see the world through the eyes of someone else.

To achieve these things, you will need to listen at least as much as you talk. Use pauses and silences to create thinking time. Focus on building and maintaining empathy. Do not confuse dialogue with decision-making – each has a different purpose that requires a different mindset. If you need a decision, leave it for another time.

Dialogue is your way of building rapport, empathy and common thought processes with your audience. By doing so, they will start to trust you and, because they know how you think and work, they will naturally turn to you more and more when they need help or input. This is your way of helping them meet your needs – make dialogue a tool in your armoury.

The right time

Choose your timing wisely. Make sure your audience has the time to enter into a dialogue with you, that they are in the right frame of mind to discuss the subject in hand and that they are prepared. If, for example, someone is rushing off to an important meeting, just about to catch a plane or focused on a key issue they are wrestling with, trying to communicate with them on a totally unrelated subject is probably not a good idea. Their attention will be focused on the subject or task in hand and your message will simply wash over them. You will either get an ill-considered response or none at all and any information you convey will, in all probability, be instantly forgotten. So ensure that neither the receiver nor you are rushed. You may wish to help prime them by sending some pre-reading material; if you do this, keep it short and very clear.

The right place

Noisy, public areas may not be the best environments for some discussions. Sometimes it may be best to converse on neutral territory. Lifts, corridors, car parks and bathrooms may again not be the right environment for many discussions. On the other hand, a less formal environment, such as a wine bar or a coffee bar, may be the best place for some tricky discussions about an interpersonal issue with a colleague or a sensitive negotiation. Ask yourself whether the subject under discussion lends itself to a formal or informal environment. Where would be quiet and free of interruptions? What resources and or facilities might you need? How much time do you need? If it can wait, which day, or time of day, would be best?

The right medium

Some messages are simple to convey while others are complex. Some may be contentious or touch on sensitivities. You may have heard stories of people being fired by text message or being dumped by a former boyfriend or girlfriend via a 'post-it note' attached to the screen of their PC. Consider what communication medium would be most appropriate in your situation: face to face, telephone, email, letter, text and so on. How does the receiver like to be communicated with? Extroverts tend to prefer face-to-face or telephone communication, and introverts prefer written. What is practical given the constraints of time and geography?

Be clear as to the purpose of your communication

You need to be clear in your own mind about the intention of your communication and the outcome(s) you would like to elicit. If you, as the sender of the message, are not clear about this, then sure as eggs are eggs, your receiver certainly will not be. The content of your messages needs to be clear, unambiguous, relevant and appropriate to the outcome you want. If, for example, you felt a member of your team was spending too long perfecting a report, tell them just that. Explain the 80–20 rule i.e. 80 per cent of the outcome is achieved from 20 per cent of the effort. Help them understand the concept of 'fit for purpose'. Do not simply tell them that you are unhappy with their productivity and that they should buck their ideas up. They may well interpret your meaning as the need to be even more perfect and consequently spend even longer on that report. Be open and honest, even if the truth is uncomfortable, and check for understanding.

See Chapter 25 for advice on listening skills. Speak from the heart and give real examples to back up or illustrate your point.

EMAIL COMMUNICATION

Email communication is invaluable for supporting, expanding and confirming what has been achieved verbally, but it has its limitations and will never replace face-to-face communication. People tend to be very precise with their questions and answers in email communication and it is difficult to register people's emotions. However, a few simple rules will significantly enhance the effectiveness of your messages:

- Ask yourself: 'Is this the most effective method of communication for this particular message?' This means considering the sensitivity of your message, the receiver's communication preferences and their physical proximity.

- Get the length right – extroverts write and prefer short conversational-style emails, whereas introverts write and prefer longer and more comprehensive emails. Extroverts may only read an email until the point they think they know what you are writing about; they will stop there and take whatever action they think appropriate. Therefore, it is wise to restrict your emails to one question only when dealing with extroverts, as any subsequent questions are likely to go unread.

- Use an effective tone – i.e. consider how your message may come across to the reader. Could it, for example, appear abrupt and cold or alternatively overly familiar? With email communication you haven't got body language to soften a blow or harsh word or a smile to indicate 'don't take this the wrong way'. Tone is the personal touch that compels a reader to react positively or negatively. An effective tone will encourage cooperation and consideration. An ineffective tone will do exactly the opposite. Consider the following examples:

    - 'I am mailing you to remind you about our follow-up meeting scheduled for tomorrow at 11 am. Last time we met you kept me waiting for 20 minutes; I do not expect to be kept waiting this time.'

    - 'I just wanted to check that we are still OK for tomorrow at 11 am. I appreciate that you are very busy and wish to thank you for your time. I understand that you have many back-to-back meetings so please let me know if you need to adjust the time of our follow-up.'

How would you respond if you received either of the above?

Finally, always remember to read your mails before you hit the send button and never fire off a response in the heat of the moment. If in doubt, save a draft and read it again tomorrow.

9 THE ART OF INFLUENCING

WHY IS THIS IMPORTANT?

The ability to influence is a key skill in any organisational setting. When you are managing projects across departmental boundaries, it is the key tool in your armoury for making things happen. Influence is the ability to bring others to your way of thinking without force or coercion; it is about genuinely winning people's support and commitment to do things because you have convinced them that it is the right or best course of action. It is about getting people to willingly do things for you or support a course of action.

Simply telling people to do something usually does not work. You may get something out of your staff by exerting position power, but you certainly will not get the best out of them. If you try to tell colleagues, peers, customers or suppliers what to do, your need is likely to go to the bottom of their list while damaging your relationship with them in the process.

Influencing people makes almost any job easier, whether it is trying to convince your boss to buy a software tool or wanting to heal relationships with disgruntled stakeholders. It generates momentum and enables your organisation to move towards its goals in a positive way.

DELVING A LITTLE DEEPER INTO THE SUBJECT

The first and very important thing to understand is that being right is generally not enough to win people over to your idea. In order to get people on your side, you have to be heard, understood, believed, offer a compelling message, demonstrate that you believe in what you are saying through passion and create motivational energy.

The American diplomat and political scientist, Henry Kissinger, once said,

> Before I served as a consultant to Kennedy, I had believed, like most academics, that the process of decision-making was largely intellectual and all one had to do was walk into the President's office and convince him of the correctness of one's view. This perspective I soon realised is as dangerously immature as it is widely held.
>
> (Fineman et al. 2005)

You need to keep in mind that you are selling both yourself and your message or idea. People need to believe in you and the message you are selling. Together they will reinforce each other and become a winning combination. Remember, 'dislike of the salesperson' is the most significant reason for not buying a product or service offered.

HINTS AND TIPS

Speak their language

In order to influence someone, you need to be able to communicate with them in their preferred language (see Chapter 8).

- For the pragmatic types you need proof and evidence, and to answer the what, when, where and how questions.

- For the theoretical types you need to make intellectual sense and answer the big 'Why?' question.

- For the idealistic types you need to illustrate a vision of a better future and demonstrate your own commitment to this vision.

- For the sociable types you need to show you understand the implications of your proposed plan for each and every person concerned and address any concerns or fears that they may have.

The theoretical types are probably the most difficult to influence; however, they are also statistically the most common type at senior levels within an organisation. Therefore it is quite important to learn the art of communicating with them and understand their language. You will need to strike a fine balance between having an opinion yourself while allowing your audience to have an input to the decision. Theorists have lots of ideas and like to have the final say – if you try to force them down a predefined path, no matter how sound your reasoning, they are likely to disagree on principle – it is the 'not invented here' syndrome. So, have an opinion, but give them room to manoeuvre, to have input and to make the idea, strategy or plan, theirs. Then you will have won them over.

Your message

You need to consider the content of your message. Think about what you are trying to achieve, what message you want to leave the other party with and what you want them to do. Your message needs to be punchy, pithy, poignant and powerful. It also needs to be simple, unambiguous and have a lasting impact. It needs to be both believable and compelling – i.e. within the bounds of possibility – while also being powerfully irresistible. Consider the following three examples:

- 'Our world-leading expertise will double your business, save your marriage and make your children clever and charming, all for the price of a cup of tea.'

  This is compelling but not believable.

- 'Our capability in this area is OK. It is as good as the competitor's and it costs about the same.'

  This is believable but not compelling.

- 'We are not the cheapest, but we are the best. If you have a breakdown we will refund up to 12 months' service fees and pay the service fees for a further 12 months from a service provider of your choice.'

This is both compelling and believable.

In addition, there are three further essential ingredients to help sell your message to your audience:

- You must yourself believe in the message you are conveying; if you do not, neither will your audience.
- Be enthusiastic – enthusiasm is contagious, so let it rub off on your audience.
- Be confident – even when you do not have the authority to make a certain decision, do not let it stop you suggesting that a change should be made.

Be honest

And last but not least, always be honest. If you are asked a question and do not know the answer say so; do not try to blag your way out of it. You will gain far more respect and credibility by being honest and straightforward.

REFERENCE

Fineman, S., Sims, D. and Gabriel, Y. (2005) *Organizing and organizations*. London and Thousand Oaks, CA: SAGE Publications Ltd.

10 REPORTS AND PRESENTATIONS

WHY IS THIS IMPORTANT?

Once you become a manager, report writing and presentation preparation is highly likely to become a greater part of your role. You may have been asked in the past to contribute to reports or presentations, but now you may be required to prepare them from scratch for delivery by either you or your boss. The purpose of these reports or presentations is likely to be one of influence towards a certain course of action or approval on a certain matter. Alternatively, their purpose may be to inform people and gain their acceptance, agreement or commitment. When a new IT initiative is conceived, the first step is likely to be a report or presentation to get the go ahead to move forward.

DELVING A LITTLE DEEPER INTO THE SUBJECT

Report writing and presentation preparation can be very time-consuming and soul-destroying when the fruits of your labour do not achieve the desired effect.

Reports and presentations are just another form of communication (see Chapter 8 for more on this) and therefore need to be tailored to the receiver. The following hints and tips will help you focus your efforts on what is important and increase the impact of your 'words'.

HINTS AND TIPS

Presentations

In this section, I will initially focus on how to tailor presentations to the individual types as described in Chapter 8 and then I will consider how best to deal with mixed audiences – a bit like first teaching you to play four different musical instruments and then how to put them together to form an orchestra.

In Chapter 8, I divided the population into four types of people – the pragmatist, the theorist, the idealist and the sociable. Each of these four types responds best to a very different presentation style suited to their own personality type.

Presenting to pragmatic types

Pragmatic types like you to be organised and structured, practical and realistic and to work logically and systematically through your analysis. They appreciate proven facts and data, empirical evidence and precise language. They like bullet point lists, graphs and charts.

This means the axes of your graphs need to be labelled properly and the numbers need to add up. If there is any error in the maths your whole presentation will lose credibility.

Pragmatic types want all the relevant information, but only relevant information, not data just lobbed in for good measure. If you have done the job properly, the answer should pop out as a logical QED conclusion – there should be no question.

When presenting to pragmatic types, you are aiming for both completeness and accuracy. Prepare your audience, i.e. start with an agenda and tell them what you are going to tell them then tell them it, ensuring you stick to your agenda. Conclude by summarising what you have just told them and ensure they understand what you require them to do with the information they have just received. Allow them space to ask questions. This style is exemplified in Figure 10.1.

Figure 10.1 Style of presentation for the pragmatic types

1. Start with an agenda

2. Work logically and systematically through your analysis
   - 2.1 *Show me that it works*
   - 2.2 *Indicate how it saves time and money*
   - 2.3 *Demonstrate a good cost-to-benefit ratio*
   - 2.4 *Show how the results can be measured*
   - 2.5 *Offer specific applications and benefits*

3. Conclude with a summary and recommendation(s)

4. Answer all my questions

5. Allow me to try it before I buy it

Presenting to theoretical types

Theoretical types value sound theories, things that appeal to their intellect and imagination, strength of character and confidence. You will gain their attention by presenting your idea in one simple, powerful, clever and ingenious model such as the two by two matrix illustrated in Figure 10.2. Your model, if it is a good one, will not need much explanation; the message should be clear and obvious.

Theoretical types do not like bullet point lists; indeed, it is the quickest and surest way to send them to sleep. Theoretical types just want the big picture, the bottom line or the conclusion. They think in threes and tend to have a very short attention span.

Make your presentation interactive and allow your theoretical types to air their opinion or concerns and to have input into your strategy or plan.

One point to bear in mind with regard to this is that theorists have a tendency to ask awkward questions to test you out. They may dive into some piece of detail, not because they are interested in the detail in its own right, but to examine your thought processes. They will want to ensure that you have done your homework, that you know your material and that your data is sound. So, be prepared with back-up material, but only use it when asked the challenging question. If you pass the test, one question is probably all you will get; if you fail the test they will go for the jugular.

This style is exemplified in the model illustrated in Figure 10.2 where:

- If you have both personal credibility and grounding in theory you will be making sense to the theoretical type – this is your goal.
- If you have personal credibility, but no grounding in theory, they will view you as a 'showman' lacking in substance.
- If you have sound theory, but no personal credibility, they are likely to think that you stole the idea from somebody else.
- If you have neither personal credibility nor grounding in theory, you will probably be perceived as 'a waste of space'.

You will note that, unlike a graph, the two axis are mutually independent of each other.

Figure 10.2 Style of presentation for the theoretical types

	Pertinent		
Grounding in theory	**Who did you steal that idea from?**	**Makes sense**
	Waste of space	**Good show but no substance**
	Irrelevant		
	Low	**Your credibility**	High

Presenting to idealistic types

Idealistic types like metaphor, analogies and imagery. Like the theorist, they are bi- picture people, but, unlike the theoretical types, they are driven by values rather than logic. Therefore, you must find out about and engage with their personal values and show how your ideas or strategies will contribute to the 'greater good' of human kind.

Demonstrate how your proposal will enhance relationships and how it will play to people's strengths and help them grow. Involve them in the process because they are ideas people too. Do not give them too much detail or shower them with facts and data – they think in threes, just like the theoretical types.

Find a metaphor or an analogy to make your point. Use pictures rather than too many words to explain your message. Once you have made your point through your metaphor or analogy, link it back to the real situation, really working that metaphor or analogy. Be passionate and enthusiastic in your delivery and inject a little humour.

This style is exemplified in Figure 10.3.

Figure 10.3 Style of presentation for the idealistic types

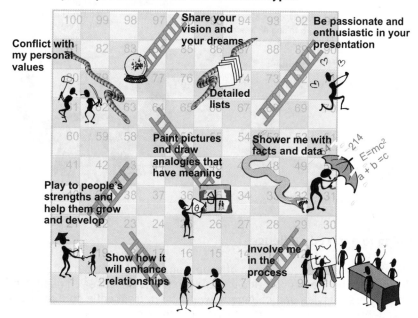

Presenting to sociable types

Sociable types like detail, but detail about people. They value the personal touch, and they want you to demonstrate how each and every individual will benefit from your proposals.

Sociable types tend to be people who really understand what is happening on the ground so take the opportunity to learn from them – make your presentation interactive and ask specific questions. Be open and straightforward, do not use implied meaning or ask rhetorical questions; keep it informal and relaxed.

Talk about Fred, Joe and Harry rather than the vague and impersonal concept of 'human resources'. Give anecdotal evidence and real stories about real people to support your recommendations. Show them respect; sociable types are the best at sensing if you are lying, patronising or railroading them, so be honest and sincere. This style is exemplified in Figure 10.4.

Figure 10.4 Style of presentation for the sociable types

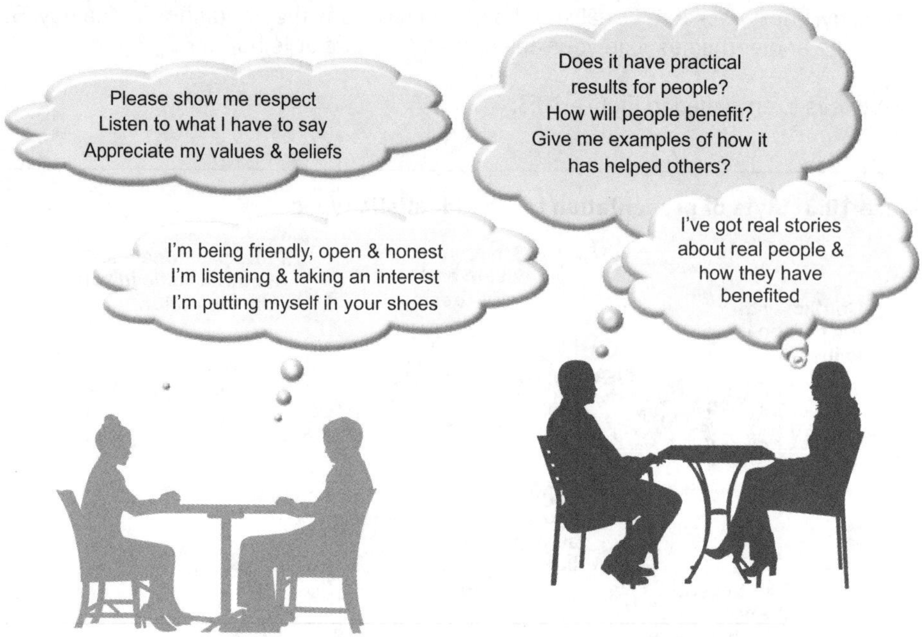

Presenting to a mixed audience

Most presentations will be to a group of people and therefore it is most probable that you will be presenting to a mixed audience. When this is the case you need to mix and match the different styles and change between them frequently so that you are not disengaging three-quarters of your audience for too long.

This means you need to give lists and data from research projects for the pragmatic types, models and theories for the theoretical types, pictorial analogies and metaphors for the idealistic types and stories about real people and how they have benefited for the sociable types.

I would recommend that you start with the style suitable for the most senior person in the room or the key decision maker. Alternatively, you may consider starting with the style suited to the majority of your audience.

> Statistically you will find pragmatists to be the most common type in professions such as IT, engineering and accountancy. If you are presenting to a senior management team or a group of marketers the most common type is likely to be theorists. Professions such as journalism, psychology and entertainment attract the idealistic type. The sociable types tend to be prevalent in the caring, hospitality and administrative professions.

Report writing

In this section I will briefly consider report writing. My focus will be on the executive summary since this is the part of the report that tends to be treated as an afterthought and gets minimal attention. However, it is the most important part of any report and in all probability will determine its success or failure. Most (70 per cent according to my own research) senior executives tend to be big picture people (the theoretical types, as described in Chapter 8) and are highly likely to only read the executive summary. At best, and only if you truly inspire them, they may then skim through a little of the body of the report. If the executive summary does not hit the spot, all the effort dedicated towards the body of the report will have been wasted.

The executive summary must be a genuine summary of the whole of the report; it must be sufficient for a busy executive to grasp the issue and make a decision. The executive summary is not an alternative term for an introduction. Executive summaries should:

- Establish the purpose of the report and why it is important or of interest.
- Summarise the current status in relation to the topic under discussion.
- Explain precisely what your key message and/or findings are.
- State what you want to happen and what actions you want taken, by whom and by when.
- Be written for someone who is very busy, and also very impatient.
- Answer the questions 'What's the point?' and 'What do I do with this information?'. This means you need to apply the 'so what?' test to everything you write.

THE 'SO WHAT' TEST

Consider the following statement: 'By ... we will have the most up-to-date technology.' The reader of such a statement could easily say 'so what?'. Your reader wants to know what benefit the new technology will provide, the impact on the bottom line, how it would improve sales opportunities or provide a competitive edge and so on. You need to answer the question for your reader 'What does it mean for me?'.

If sufficiently excited by the executive summary, your reader may dip into the body of the report. Make the reading easy for them and make it inviting; use space, structure, bullet points, bold type, numbering, short sentences, plain English, paragraphs and so on. Use diagrams, graphs and pictures to illustrate key points and break the text up; as the saying goes 'a picture is worth a thousand words'. Focus on what adds value and remove anything that does not add to your message. Expand acronyms, set the context and do not use technical jargon unless the entire readership understands it.

Text that is too dense, littered with jargon and three letter acronyms and contains long convoluted sentences is the quickest and easiest way to switch a reader off.

Put key messages in section headings. This will provide two key benefits: it is likely to entice your reader to read further and, even if it does not, you will have communicated your most important points.

11 UNDERSTANDING YOUR CUSTOMERS

WHY IS THIS IMPORTANT?

Now you are a manager your focus will become more externally directed and your interactions with other business functions will increase. These business functions are your 'customers', albeit internal ones. As an IT function your prime reason for being is as a service provider to these customers. Customers are your reason for being; without them you would not exist. Your aim, therefore, should be to delight your customers and to become their supplier of choice (even if they do not have a choice).

In order to become the supplier of choice you will need to:

1. exceed expectations;
2. be easy to deal with, i.e. to do business with.

DELVING A LITTLE DEEPER INTO THE SUBJECT

It is far more difficult to please customers of a service offering than those of a product offering. We expect services to work and when they do we do not give them a second thought; however, when they go wrong we are very quick to kick and scream. Therefore, when delivering a service offering, you will have to work twice as hard to delight your customers in comparison with someone with a product offering.

The typical IT professional is driven more by intellectual curiosity than a desire to serve. They get frustrated by customers who do not know what they want, who cannot make up their mind and who change priorities causing plans to be redrawn. They have a desire to pin requirement down to the nth degree as soon as possible, so they can get onto the real and interesting work: the intellectual challenge of getting the technology to do what they want it to do and pushing the boundaries of what is technically possible. Many IT people are excited by the technology itself, whereas their customers tend to be interested in what the technology can do for them. As a marketeer would say, 'people don't buy drills, they buy holes'.

By way of an analogy, consider a motorcar. A feature of that motorcar may be that it has a large engine; the advantage of that large engine is that it allows you to drive quickly, but this only translates into a benefit if you want to go quickly. Road safety, fuel economy or space for luggage and kids, for example, may be far more important to you than speed. The trick is to think in terms of benefits rather than features.

In the world of IT, people are very good at thinking in terms of features, as these are tangible; however, the result is often technology for the sake of technology. Consider Microsoft's 'Office'™ product for example – what percentage of its features do you use on a daily basis? For most people it is probably less than 10 per cent. Only a small minority will be excited about the technology and its possibilities in their own right.

Thinking benefits requires the ability to put yourself in the shoes of your customer and understand things from their perspective. The added complication is that benefits are often woolly, intangible things like 'peace of mind', 'feeling important' and 'being able to hand everything over to someone else'.

IT people are often scornful of marketeers, accusing them of trying to sell people something that they do not need. The irony here is that IT people are far more guilty of trying to do this than most marketeers, who have long discovered that their job is far more about identifying and meeting real needs and wants than it is about trying to create artificial needs and wants.

HINTS AND TIPS

Many years ago, as a business analyst, I was taught to differentiate between customer wants and needs. The latter were to be addressed, but the former were to receive a polite rejection. There are two issues with this approach. First, establishing what the needs are can be difficult as customers often do not really know themselves what their needs are and IT professionals are generally very bad at second-guessing. Second, you need to appreciate that customer 'wants' have emotional elements and if these are not addressed satisfactorily it can lead to dissatisfied and complaining customers. So how do you find out what your customer really, really wants?

My first and very important piece of practical advice is to talk to your customers and spend time with them so that you really get to understand their business and develop a trust-based relationship (see Chapter 14 for more on relationship building). Use their language, i.e. business language, rather than your language, i.e. IT jargon. This must be an ongoing dialogue throughout the life of the project. This is important as requirements will change – which is not the customers' 'fault', but rather a reflection that businesses are constantly changing. You need to ask the right questions in the right way to help your customers think through what is important to them – they may not know this until you draw it out of them.

What often happens is that those in IT make an assumption about what their customer wants because they think they know the answer and are itching to get on with the task in hand. Alternatively, they do ask but let their customer do part of their job for them. Let me explain:

- Business people are great at presuming solutions to business problems and when these solutions involve technology they are inevitably ill-conceived. It is a case of 'a little knowledge can be a dangerous thing'.

- Because they are the customer, IT professionals often take what they are asking for at face value and do their very best to comply, even if the request is ill-conceived.

- Ultimately what has been asked for is delivered and, to IT's surprise and disappointment, the customer is less than delighted because it was not what was needed. It is often at this point that customers understand what they really wanted in the first place.

- The result is wasted time, wasted money, wasted effort, frustration and disappointment. In addition, relationships and reputations will suffer, making it even more challenging to do business together in the future.

So, the main thing for you as an IT manager is to get out there and talk to your customers and find out what is really important to them. In order to do this you need to go beyond their stated 'wants' and ask questions such as:

- Why do you want it?
- What will it do for you?
- How will it improve things?
- What will it enable you to do differently?

Your tone needs to be friendly and interested, and your questions need to be 'open' rather than 'closed'. A closed question is one that can be answered with a simple yes or no, whereas an open question necessitates a fuller response. Use silence to encourage deeper thought, and ultimately summarise what you have heard and understood, but beware of closing down too soon. Ask 'clean' questions rather than 'dirty' ones – dirty questions are leading questions whereby you encourage the other person to give the answer you want.

Once you understand what your customer wants, it is time to use your knowledge, past experiences and intuition to suggest ways of addressing that need. Giving your customers a choice of appropriate solutions enables them to own the outcome rather than being told what it should be. The following case study provides a good illustration of this advice.

The IT director of a retail bank was asked one day to extend their services to a 24×7 operation. This was neither practical nor feasible, but instead of saying 'no' or giving an exorbitant estimate the IT director used the questioning techniques just described to ascertain the driver behind this request. She asked her banking director customer why he wanted 'to go 24×7'. The banking director explained that the bank had been the first telephone bank and for a couple of years this had been their unique selling proposition (USP); however, many other banks had subsequently followed suit. The banking director felt that the bank now needed a new USP and he saw a 24×7 operation as providing this.

The IT director then asked him a number of questions to find out what exactly he was trying to achieve – i.e. if he wanted to offer a full service throughout the night – what volumes he anticipated, whether the data needed to be 'up to the minute' or whether it would matter if it were a few hours old and so on. Armed with the answers to these questions the IT director was able to suggest an alternative solution: downloading the data at 6 p.m. each evening onto a large PC and running a basic enquiry service overnight until the main systems came back online at 8 a.m. the following morning. The banking director liked the idea of trialling such a quick and simple solution.

Over the subsequent three-month trial period they monitored the volumes and type of activity. Armed with this information the banking director made a somewhat different business decision. He decided to offer the full banking services, but only between the hours of 7 a.m. and 9 p.m. seven days per week. Managers would work shifts, allowing complex decisions on loans and so on to be made. The trial, and the data collected from it, had enabled the business to make a wiser decision than was previously possible. IT had exceeded expectations and delighted their customer, and the IT director became the heroine rather than the villain.

Asking questions, when done skilfully, brings mutual benefits. It helps your customer to think through what is important to them and helps you to get a much clearer picture of the kind of world your customer wants to inhabit and how IT can help create that world. Done badly, however, and it can appear intrusive, overly personal and patronising.

Equally important in this respect is being 'easy to deal with'. Consider how you feel when you get passed from pillar to post with a question or concern about a product or service. How irritated you feel when you have to listen to automated menu after menu, none of the choices are appropriate and it seems impossible to get to speak to a human being, and then, just when you think you have got somewhere, you are asked to put it in writing or to complete a 10-page form.

Some things that might help include:

- Be available to speak with on the phone or face to face, minimise form filling and, if forms are required, fill them in for your customer.

- Take responsibility for finding the right person that someone needs to talk to or for resolving the issue yourself – willingly take the monkey on your back and do not expect your customers to try to find their way around your IT function.

- Streamline processes and minimise the bureaucracy. Question the way things are done, and ask 'what is the purpose of this check and balance?'. Does it add real value or do you do it because you have always done it?

12 MANAGING AND NEGOTIATING WITH SUPPLIERS

WHY IS THIS IMPORTANT?

As a manager, your focus will become more externally directed and this will include dealing with suppliers. The more IT becomes commoditised the more suppliers you will have to deal with. It is written in folklore that suppliers, and indeed consultants, are the big bad wolf. Do not trust them is the message from the past. However, more recent evidence suggests that adversarial relationships like these are ineffective. You might achieve a short-term gain, but destroy any prospect of good will in the future. The name of the game is mutual benefit, which will entail cooperation and a desire to reach a deal that is good for both parties.

DELVING A LITTLE DEEPER INTO THE SUBJECT

I have a friend who used to be a top IBM salesperson; she is now a top CIO head-hunter. Her advice is to build win–win relationships with your suppliers. She tells me that, when she was in her sales role, all the customers that she had a good relationship with got all of the deals and offers, got the first call on the best people and when problems occurred were always top of the priority list for resolution. Those she did not have a good relation-ship with were always bottom of the list and got the dregs of what was left over.

Poorly treated suppliers, especially those whose profits may be under threat by hard negotiations on your part, will deliver a poorer service. They may well do what you ask of them and deliver to contract, but you will get the bare minimum, you will be bottom of their priority list and you will be the last to be offered any deals or given the heads up on any offers or new offerings.

> Treat your relationship with your suppliers as a partnership; your goal should be to achieve a win–win relationship. If you treat your suppliers right they are far more likely to treat you right.

HINTS AND TIPS

First of all, you need to be very clear and honest about what you want from a supplier. They are providing a service, and you are paying for it. But this takes us back to drills and holes; you are not buying a service from them, you are buying what that service can deliver.

Take, for example, one classic use of consultants: your CEO will not listen to you so you delve into your consultancy budget, hire a big name and tell them exactly what you want them to say to the CEO, which is what you have been trying to say for years. In go the consultants and, frustrating though it is, achieve in one presentation what you have been trying to achieve for months, years maybe.

In this case, what are you buying? It is clearly not expertise or knowledge and neither is it the 'right answer', as you have provided all of these. What you are buying from them is 'credibility'. In marketing speak this is termed the 'value proposition' or, in plain English, the things someone wants from spending their money. Things like 'holes in kitchen walls', 'peace of mind when driving my family' (for Volvo drivers) and 'being recognised as having style' (for some designer label wearers) are all examples of value propositions.

So, understanding what you want from a supplier is very important. It is often when buyer and supplier have different perceptions of the value proposition that disappointment and lack of trust arise.

You might, for example, be looking for contract staff, but what is your underlying value proposition? Are you, say, in need of:

- A safe pair of hands?

- An expert (because you are lacking a certain skill)?

- A teacher and coach who will develop your own people?

Just like you and your service to your customers, your supplier will be measured, ultimately, not on the overt terms and conditions of the contract, but on how they deliver to the underlying value proposition.

This means you need a clear and mutual understanding of the value proposition in terms of outcomes and not inputs. Establish good personal relationships with your suppliers and treat them with respect and honesty. Keep an open dialogue. This will ensure that misunderstandings do not occur and will ultimately form the basis of a true partnership. The chances are that at least part of the value proposition will only be possible and become apparent when you meet regularly and talk freely.

Developing partnerships

At the beginning of any relationship with a supplier it is important that you induct them into your organisation, helping them to understand your business.

You also need to consider your choice of supplier, asking questions such as:

- Are they the right type of supplier to fulfil your need?

- Is there cultural compatibility between your organisations?

- What is their size in relation to you?

- How significant is the deal for them – are you going to be a big fish in a small pond or vice versa?

Negotiating

You will need to hone your negotiating skills. To be successful in negotiating you need to be both assertive and cooperative. Be open about your position and be understanding of your supplier's position. Put things on the table and be open to alternatives.

For example, your supplier may not be in a position to reduce the price, but they may be able to give you something else; something that is of significant value to you, but costs them little, such as throwing in a year's worth of maintenance for free. The more flexible you are, the more options and routes you leave open for your negotiation to take, and the greater chance you have of getting something that works for you.

Conceding something will also make you appear more amenable and will encourage your supplier to be more generous in other areas. It may be worth having a concession or two up your sleeve in advance.

Use all the advice on communication and influencing described in Chapters 8 and 9. Develop your political acumen (see Chapter 22) and your emotional intelligence (see Chapter 25) and you will become a great negotiator. Always keep the aim of win–win in mind throughout any negotiation and focus on what is fair and reasonable for both parties.

On a cautionary note, be mindful of your authority levels and negotiating limits. Depending on the size, culture and maturity of your organisation, and whether you are in the private or public sector, these can range from relatively high to extremely low.

13 MANAGING YOUR BOSS

WHY IS THIS IMPORTANT?

The relationship between boss and subordinate is a two-way process. Just as you manage your team, bosses can and should be managed too. You may not have any choice about who your boss is, but you have far more control than you may think about how your boss treats you and the relationship you have with them.

The ability to manage upward is a key managerial skill and one that not only you will benefit from; your team will benefit too. As a manager you have a duty of care to your own staff to ensure you get the best out of your manager. Your boss may or may not be good at their job, clear in their communication or caring and compassionate. But one thing is for sure, they have more access to resources and more power than you – and they have a huge say in what you and your team do now, what you will do in the future, what you get paid and how much visibility you get from above them.

The IT function is not renowned for developing managerial and leadership capability, so, just as you may have had little help developing your managerial skills, the same may be also true of your boss.

Your manager may be good or bad, supportive or destructive, open and friendly or secretive and manipulative. Whatever their characteristics, they behave differently with different people. How they behave towards you depends on how you manage your interactions and how much responsibility you take for creating a positive working relationship. Just as you give feedback and delegate to others, you can use the same processes in reverse to help your boss to delegate to you and to give you helpful feedback.

If you want to get better, more interesting tasks, get promoted and get paid more, the most effective strategy is to learn to be good at managing your manager.

When you start to work positively with your manager, you start to take control of your own destiny and things are far less likely to spin out of control, produce uncomfortable surprises or simply sap your time in unnecessary re-work or politicking.

DELVING A LITTLE DEEPER INTO THE SUBJECT

The chances are that your boss is so busy reacting to events that they do not have time to think about how they can develop you and, perhaps more importantly from their point of view, how they can use you and your time to make their own life easier.

Before your boss will delegate important and interesting stuff to you, they have to learn to trust you. This is a slow process and trust is built one step at a time. Let us look at a simple example.

Your boss has just called a meeting of your entire peer group to discuss ways of cutting costs. Everyone has contributed and your boss has been left with a long list of suggestions that you know will form the basis of a report he now needs to submit to his boss. You could say, 'I know you're really busy, would it help if I wrote up all the suggestions from today to feed into your report?'

By taking this style of approach with your manager, you are achieving several things:

- You show that you are thinking and interested in what happens in the broader context.
- You show that you have an appreciation of what your boss does and that you could take some of their load.
- You will learn about how your boss thinks and what sorts of ideas they are prepared to take upwards.

By using such an approach, you can influence the sort of work that comes your way and, at the same time, build a trusting relationship with your boss.

HINTS AND TIPS

People often make the mistake of thinking that managers delegate to the person most competent and able to do the job. Yet, in most cases, they delegate to the person that they have a trust-based relationship with. Trust takes time to build and it generally does not come through showing that you are smart, able or energetic. Trust comes when you get to know someone, show them that you have the same values as they do, demonstrate personal loyalty and achieve mutual respect. Once you have a trust-based relationship it becomes easy for them to turn to you; it also allows them to let down their guard with you, to ask for help and to admit their own vulnerabilities. Interestingly, it also makes them far more likely to turn a blind eye if and when you do not perform quite as well as you should have done.

Some of you will be lucky and your relationship with your boss will develop naturally and easily; for others it will take time, effort and tenacity. Either way, the following advice will help you to build rapport and a trust-based relationship with your manager.

Get to know your boss

- **Find out what makes your boss tick.** Learn to read their moods and behaviours and the secret code embedded in their speech. What winds them up? What sparks their interest and gets them excited? Focus your conversations on what interests them rather than what bores them; if you have done something that is necessary, but you know that your boss finds it boring, just give them the headline news and move on quickly to something that they are more interested in.

- **Find out what is the most important thing to them.** Is it competence, personal reputation, quality, customer satisfaction and so on? What keeps them awake at night? Every manager has one or more hot topics that always get their instant attention. Find out what does it for your boss and then find a way of linking whatever you do or talk about back to one of your boss's hot buttons.

- Do some gentle investigation – what are the one or two **biggest successes and biggest calamities** that have happened on your boss's watch? This will provide you with valuable insights into the things you should be talking about and the sensitivities that may be best avoided – no one likes to be reminded of past mistakes.

- **Assess their personality type.** Are they a pragmatic, theoretical, idealistic or sociable boss? Once you have assessed their type, use all the advice on communication and influence in Chapters 8 and 9.

- It is also helpful to **establish some common ground**. Look for shared interests, common background or places you have lived, kids of a similar age or at the same school/university, books you have both read – anything to show that you are on the same page of life.

Your boss' management style

Help your boss to manage you in the way you like to be managed. In order to do that, it is good to think about the following:

- How much detail and guidance do you like about a task? Do you like to know exactly what is expected of you and by when, a clear methodology and check points or would you prefer a blank sheet of paper and the freedom to do it your way?

- Where do your interests and aspirations lie? What organisational activities would you like to be involved in? What skills would you like to develop? Are you more interested in becoming a generalist or a specialist? Do you like to be invited to meetings, consulted on matters, or do you just prefer to be left alone to get on with things?

- What is your preferred degree of openness? Do you want to get to know your boss personally, go for a drink after work with them, or would you prefer a more distant relationship and to keep your work and personal life totally separate?

Be open and transparent with your boss

Promote an open dialogue with your boss (see the advice in Chapter 8). Encourage your boss to engage in dialogue with you, set the tone and set the norm. In all probability your boss will follow your lead. This is where coaching skills will come into play, see Chapter 28 for advice on developing coaching skills.

Ask for feedback

It is important to know what your manager thinks of you, what pleases them most about your work, your style and approach and also what they appreciate least. The only way you will get to know is through feedback and the best way of getting feedback is to ask for it. So simply and regularly, say to your boss 'How am I doing?'. When asking for feedback, the most important thing is to make the process as easy and painless as possible, so make use of all the advice on asking for and receiving feedback in Chapter 3.

Seek coaching

One of the key things you need from your boss is coaching. They know stuff that you do not know, they have access to company information and resources that you do not and they are called upon to do things of which you do not normally have visibility. You need them to induct you into some of these mysteries and to guide and support you as you step up to new challenges. But the chances are that they are neither skilled at coaching or at diagnosing your coaching needs. So, rather than hope that they may be sent on a coaching course, you need to learn the structure and art of coaching and then subtly coach them on how to coach you. See Chapter 28 for advice on how to do this.

Give feedback

Your manager needs feedback too; without it they cannot learn and develop. They may feel embarrassed about asking you for feedback for fear of looking weak or ineffectual. This is not good for them, but it is also not good for you; if they do not get appropriate feedback, they will not have a clue about how to develop you or how to become a more effective leader themselves.

Make it your goal to understand what your boss needs to know in order to develop both you and them on your respective journeys; use the advice in Chapter 3 on giving feedback.

Giving feedback to your boss is similar to giving feedback to a member of your team, but with a little more 'ego-massaging' and deference. The most important thing to remember is that your focus is on improving your relationship with your boss and helping you both to function well together. You are not necessarily trying to make them a better person – although that might be a positive side benefit!

When you are giving feedback to your boss, make sure that you have a plan of what you want to achieve with this particular interaction. Work on the principle of one objective per meeting. The biggest single mistake that people make is to go into a meeting with a shopping list of things they want their boss to do. Focus on one issue or behaviour, get that right and move on to something else only when you are sure that your boss has got the message and is now performing to your entire satisfaction in relation to that issue or behaviour. Remember also that this is a relationship, so you need to be aware of what you say and do and how you say and do it.

If you become practised at engaging your manager in dialogue, seeking and giving honest feedback and looking for opportunities to be coached, you will find that you create a relationship with them where they just naturally seem to know what you need from them.

Build trust and demonstrate loyalty

Trust and loyalty are the foundations on which relationships are built; they are the key to becoming part of your boss's inner circle. Loyal and trusted staff are likely to be the first to find out about things; they will be confided in, asked for their views and opinions on matters and when times get tough they will find shelter under their boss's organisational umbrella. Loyalty is usually a two-way street – when you demonstrate loyalty, it tends to come back in spades.

Building trust takes time and effort and demonstrating loyalty requires a degree of selflessness. You have to be there for people when they need you most, rather than when it is beneficial or convenient for you.

> Lots of people want to ride with you in the limo, but what you want is someone who will take the bus with you when the limo breaks down.
>
> Oprah Winfrey

Being loyal to your boss or your organisation is about looking out for them, making sure that they do the right thing, and protecting their back when others waiver in their commitment to a course of action that they know to be right, but do not have the courage, stamina, focus or energy to follow through on. Loyalty involves being supportive and helpful and above all not being critical, gossiping or saying and doing anything that might undermine your boss or your organisation.

In public you always speak well of your boss and, if need be, you defend their actions. In private it is your job and your duty to give them feedback to challenge the ethical and moral grounds of their actions and decisions and to help them reflect on the outcomes of their actions so that they can develop into a better boss and a more effective business leader. Share things with them that you hear said about their style or decisions – they will not necessarily have the right feedback channels to discover these things in other ways.

14 RELATIONSHIP MANAGEMENT

WHY IS THIS IMPORTANT?

No man is an island.

John Donne (1572–1631)

We need the support of others to flourish both socially and organisationally. Relationships are the foundations of everything we do; they are the gateway to being heard and respected. Without effective relationships with your peer group you are unlikely to get the opportunity to voice your ideas or suggestions, even if they are the greatest in the world. You are also unlikely to be able to get people to cooperate when you ask them to do things; you will need the input from others in order to get things done and to make your projects a success. If you have the right relationships, that input will be easy to obtain and offered willingly; if you do not have the right relationships, progress will be impeded, if not halted, and frustrations will set in.

The more people know, respect, like and trust you, the more cooperation you will get and the speedier their response will be. If you do not know, respect, like or trust someone their request tends to go to the bottom of the pile.

DELVING A LITTLE DEEPER INTO THE SUBJECT

It can be very frustrating when initiatives grind to a halt – whether that is because a crucial sign-off is not given, you cannot get time in someone's diary to talk about their requirements or a key stakeholder does not turn up to a project review meeting.

If someone reports directly to you, you can use position power, if need be, to enforce action; however, if they do not it is a lot trickier. In that case, your prime tools are your relationship with them, your reputation and your ability to influence.

Consider the following story.

My career commenced within the shipbuilding industry. It was the early 1980s and I joined a shipyard along with nine other engineering graduates. I spent the first two years on the shop floor as a 'fitter's mate' in order to complete my training to become a chartered engineer. During this time I learned little about engineering, but a lot about people, industrial relations and shop-floor survival tactics.

Following my stint on the shop floor, I went into the planning department and quickly became involved with the very first rollout of computers onto the shop floor. I was appointed to manage two major projects; the first was a manufacturing control system that I affectionately named COMICS (computer-oriented manufacturing information and control system), and the second was an access-control system whereby entry to or exit from the shipyard could only be gained via a bank of 20 computer-controlled turnstiles.

At this point in my life and career, I was naïvely unaware of the potential human and social problems that I now know are a characteristic of any project that seeks to change long-established and cherished ways of working. I was also unaware of the stages a computing project should go through, the development life cycle or the existence of development methodologies; I therefore operated purely on instinct, gut feeling and basic common sense.

And yet both projects were a huge success. I cannot claim they went in on time, to budget or as specified since there was no budget, plan or detailed specification. However, the systems worked – they fulfilled business imperatives, the workforce liked them and the unions were content. Over the period of time covered by these projects, I was promoted three times, my salary doubled and I became the youngest manager in the history of the shipyard.

As my career progressed, I learned how to manage projects and develop systems 'properly'. It was at this point in my career that things started to go downhill. Don't get me wrong, I never did a bad job, but I could never recapture my early successes. The question is why?

As I look back over this time, my analysis of the situation is as follows. As my career progressed, I moved away from engineering and became a fully fledged member of the IT community, and in doing so I also moved to the finance sector where money was more plentiful and business was booming. I was sent on training courses; I learned about methodologies, process and procedures and project management. I watched my peers and bosses, learned from them and tried to emulate their behaviour. However, somewhere along the way I forgot what came naturally to me – the people side, networking and building relationships!

During the early part of my career I had naturally (for me, that is) focused on building relationships with people. I did this throughout my two-year stint on the shop floor. I got to know people, I made friends, I made myself useful, I helped people out, I stuck up for them when they were treated unfairly and I took an interest in people and their work. Later, when I talked to the people on the shop floor and to the unions, I was not viewed as an outsider, I was one of them and trusted because we had a common experience and understood each other's values. When I told them that the implementation of the IT systems wouldn't threaten their jobs, but would ease some of the more mundane aspects, they believed me and willingly helped my projects happen.

During the middle years of my career, I learned to consider the time I had spent on relationship building as a luxury rather than as a necessity. I therefore stopped doing it because I didn't feel I had the time; I felt that I should be concentrating on 'work'. Lunch breaks became a snatched sandwich while catching up with my email rather than dining with, talking to and getting to know the people who would be impacted by my endeavours: my stakeholders and business peers.

With the wisdom that comes with age, and the benefit of hindsight, I now understand where I went wrong; how I had ignored a natural and oh so important talent of mine – that of relationship building.

Relationship building comes more naturally to some people than others. The good news, however, is that it is a skill that can be learned. The key message from this chapter is to never underestimate, or lose sight of, the importance of relationships!

I recently undertook a major study of IT professionals who have progressed beyond the ranks of IT and made it to the position of CEO. Such individuals told me that they spent 50 per cent of their time networking and relationship building while in that top IT role. As one of the CEOs in my study so succinctly put it, 'IT leadership is about getting the best out of people and not about building processes and procedures'.

HINTS AND TIPS

So, how do you go about building relationships with 'strangers' within your organisation? The following tactics will all help, but I suggest that you start by choosing one or two ideas and building them into the way you do things. Once these have become embedded as good habits, revisit the list and choose two more areas to work on and so on.

- Always speak well of others; never denigrate anyone behind their back. If you say something bad about someone to someone else, how does that someone else know that you are not doing the same to them behind their back?

- Take an interest in other people. For most people, their favourite topic is either themselves or the achievements of members of their family. Listen carefully; this is how you get to know someone and find out about their values and what is important to them. Try and remember some basics about them, their partner's name, the ages of their children, what pets they own and so on, to show wider interest than just the job – be prepared to share similar details about yourself.

- Develop the ability to converse on a wide range of subjects – your aim is to show that you know just enough about what people are saying to recognise that they are making a really valuable contribution, and to be able to ask meaningful questions that give them the opportunity to impress you some more. Resist the temptation to show them how much you know on the topic.

- Look for common interests – these will always provide an easy, non-threatening ice-breaker on any occasion.

- Actively listen to others and accept that they have a valid point of view, even if you do not agree with it. If you can learn how they see the world, and why they see it like they do, you will be better placed to understand their behaviour, the decisions they make and assess how you can help each other.

- Praise rather than criticise and never, ever argue with someone. You cannot win an argument. If you lose you have lost and if you win you have lost because you have just created a grievance in the mind of the other person and potentially destroyed any chance of building a positive relationship.

- Demonstrate empathy and sensitivity to the moods and feelings of others. You need to engage emotionally as well as intellectually.

- Respect and value people for who they are, warts and all, without trying to change them. Delight in their idiosyncrasies and peculiarities rather than trying, commonly in vain, to mould them into some ideal or norm.

- Demonstrate modesty and humility and be prepared to admit your mistakes or that you are wrong. Develop your sense of humour and your ability to laugh at yourself.

- Put yourself out to help others without expecting anything in return.

Make it your mission to give a little to the people you come across each day who are generally ignored by the masses, such as security guards, car-park attendants, cleaners, drivers, receptionists and so on. Acknowledge their existence by saying 'hello', 'good morning' or 'good evening' and engage in a little small talk. Look for an opportunity to compliment or thank them. People like to feel valued for who they are and what they do and people in such professions are vital, but rarely noticed or acknowledged. They have their own network and pretty soon word will get around – 'that one is OK', 'he's not stuck up like the rest', 'she made my day'. Remember that value can come out of the most unlikely acquaintanceships.

This advice will require you to be generous with yourself and your time, but remember you never know what you might need from someone in the future. A little act of random kindness will also leave you with that 'feel good' factor and is therefore a win-win in itself.

It is also worth noting that although this chapter focuses on workplace relationships, the same skills are just as applicable in your personal life.

PART 3
THINGS THAT YOU NEED TO UNDERSTAND, HAVE AN OPINION ON AND MAKE A CONTRIBUTION TO

15 SYSTEMS AND PROCESSES

WHY IS THIS IMPORTANT?

For the past 35 years or so IT professionals have been trying to perfect the art of managing IT projects and programmes. When I started my career in IT there were no methodologies to follow; the approach was very much a 'fly by the seat of your pants' one. Then over the years various methodologies and productivity tools were born and subsequently died. Each new generation attempted to give more control, predictability and certainty, and the pendulum swung from very little control to very tight control.

Many would argue that the pendulum has swung too far towards control, that IT management has become too rigid, too bureaucratic and that methodologies such as PRINCE2 and ITIL have slowed things down and added tedium and frustration to the working day. The pendulum has now started to swing back with Agile methodologies replacing waterfall development techniques in many organisations. The move to DevOps is looking like the next step.

In your first managerial position it is unlikely that you will be responsible for deciding what methodologies or governance structure you adopt. However, it is highly likely that you will be expected to have knowledge of the various methodologies and an opinion on their suitability for your environment. You may also be expected to give feedback on how current methodologies are working and to support the implementation of changes to those methodologies or the adoption of new methodologies.

DELVING A LITTLE DEEPER INTO THE SUBJECT

I am not going to attempt to give an analysis or summary of all the various methodologies or governance structures around. There are many books on these subjects that will give detailed and specific information (see Further Reading for some suggestions). Read up on the subject so that you have a thorough understanding of those adopted by your organisation. While reading up on specific tools or methodologies, assess their various merits and suitability for your organisation, taking into consideration the general advice given in the next section.

HINTS AND TIPS

The concept of project management

I like to use an analogy to explain the principals of project management. Put simply, managing projects is rather like flying commercial passenger aircraft, where the pilot is the project manager, air traffic control is the programme management, the cabin crew are your project team and the passengers are your stakeholders. The aim of the pilot is to launch and then successfully land the right projects on time and in budget such that the key stakeholders are satisfied. This process should, ideally, be uneventful – like projects, most people prefer their flights to be without incident. Your stakeholders are not interested in the journey itself, they just want the benefits of the destination.

Just like pilots, project managers need to be trained, prepared and in control. Pilots do not take off without doing the necessary preparation: planning (flight plan), check lists (pre-flight checks), risk management (weather) and constant monitoring and control. Pilots also have to sign off aircraft before take off and can refuse to sign if they think the risk is too high. In many organisations project managers are not given a choice in the matter and are sometimes misled about the status of the project they are expected to fly – small wonder that most projects fail or, if they do arrive, they are late, over-budget or with quality compromised.

One of the greatest concerns of pilots is the weather – in project terms 'risk'. Likewise project managers should use risk (weather) forecasting methods to ensure that risks are identified, avoided or controlled, thus ensuring as smooth a flight as possible. While forecasts and a weather eye can help avoid the worst weather conditions, there is always the possibility of the unexpected (clear air turbulence in aviation terms). Good pilots, and hence good project managers, must be capable of dealing with events that were neither planned nor forecasted. Severe weather often leads commercial pilots to fly longer routes (using more valuable fuel) in order to ensure a smooth flight. Project managers do likewise, but sometimes budget or time constraints mean that the project has to fly through turbulence and so projects can be very stressful to individuals (see Chapter 19 on how to cope with stress and pressure).

Always consider what is 'fit for purpose'

Projects, like aircraft, come in many shapes and sizes; therefore, you cannot treat all projects equally. A small project will require different treatment from a large project and a mainstream project will require different treatment from a pioneering one. The level of control needs to be fit for purpose; i.e. you want sufficient control, but you do not need an overdose.

The simple model in Figure 15.1 depicts four different types of project that you will encounter. Each type of project will require different treatment and a different level of control as described in the following section.

Figure 15.1 Project portfolio

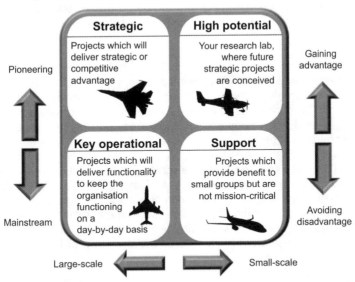

Strategic projects are akin to Concord. They are high profile projects; the ones that will make a big difference to the way your organisation functions or your competitive position within the market place. The stakes will be high and the potential rewards significant. They are high risk because they are unique; you will be leading the way without any bench mark or 'best practice' to follow.

Strategic projects will need to be carefully planned but not managed down to the nth degree. There will be many unknowns and a degree of uncertainty. Do not let the search for certainty kill the project off. You will need to exercise flexibility, common sense, sound judgement and pragmatism. Speed will be imperative. If the project is a success, others will copy it and it will cease to be unique and hence will no longer provide that strategic or competitive edge. Once this happens it will become a key operational system.

Key operational projects are akin to jumbo jets. These projects are often large, costly, of high and long-term benefit to a large group of stakeholders but similar to projects previously undertaken. They may involve the implementation of key operational systems or enhancements to ones already in place. Key operational systems are the ones keeping your organisation running efficiently and effectively on a day-by-day basis. Without them your organisation would find it very difficult to function for anything but a short period of time. These are mission-critical systems and will be similar to any other organisation in the same sector as you. They do not provide strategic advantage, but they do avoid disadvantage.

These need to be carefully planned, managed and tested; quality will be more important than speed. They will need to be built to last, so do not skimp and scrape. Most methodologies are primarily designed to handle this type of project.

Support projects are akin to 737s. These are smaller projects that are run so numerously and frequently that they almost become taken for granted. They are aimed at creating efficiencies for small work groups. They are not mission-critical – i.e. your organisation would still function without them – but there may be small-scale inefficiencies.

The number of support projects taken on will need to be tightly controlled, but there needs to be flexibility within the management of each; your objective should be lean and mean. If you do not employ adequate filtration they will eat away all your resources. You should also be wary of succumbing to the desire for a new or latest 'toy'. Treat your business colleagues as you imagine you would treat a child when they demand the latest trainers or computer game.

High-potential projects are akin to light aircraft. They carry few passengers and are free to fly virtually anywhere at their own risk. They may 'discover' new destinations, i.e. new markets or new ways of doing things. Basically, they are small experiments – you try out lots of things, spending only a little bit of time and money on each. Most will wither and die, but a few will demonstrate their potential to transform the way things are done. These new destinations will open up the skies to your large aircraft projects and become your future strategic systems.

Your control mechanisms should focus around time boxing, cost boxing or both. Apart from that, you need freedom and flexibility. You cannot do a cost–benefit analysis on the germ of an idea! Once you have a proof of concept, this is the time to move into a more formal project structure.

Focus on the purpose of each check and balance. Always focus on the benefit of the information provided by the control measurement:

- What purpose does it serve?
- What will people do with the information?
- How will it change things?
- How will it impact decision-making?
- What would happen if you did not have this information?
- Any other questions that may be relevant.

Information for the sake of information is simply pointless and a waste of time, money and effort.

Make your systems and processes easy to use and 'idiot' proof. Do not make processes or procedures complicated or time-consuming. Remove the jargon, avoid duplication and pre-fill forms as much as you can.

Be realistic. Do not nominate someone as a sponsor for a project if they do not have the time to perform the role or if they lack commitment.

Apply common sense. There are always exceptions to any rule and things that do not neatly fit into a category. Be flexible and pragmatic and allow common sense to override bureaucracy. Remember 'common sense' is often not very common at all!

Avoid game playing as far as you can. This often becomes an issue at budget time whereby departments submit inflated budgets because they know they are going to be told to reduce them, only to agree, after numerous meetings and protracted negotiations, on the sum that they had in mind at the outset. See Chapter 22 for advice on corporate politics.

Be prepared to give ballpark estimates. Common questions you may be asked frequently are, 'How long will X take?' or 'How much should be put in the budget for Y?' In all likelihood what is required is a ballpark estimate. However, many IT people feel uncomfortable with giving off-the-cuff estimates. IT people like to be accurate and precise and may well feel that they will be held to their estimate. Providing you make it clear that your estimate is simply an estimate and not a guarantee, you should be OK. Adopt the methodology of quoting high, medium or low, large, medium or small or give a range that you are comfortable with. If you delay giving an answer for two weeks while you crunch the numbers, you will only irritate and annoy and gain the reputation of being uncooperative and unimaginative.

16 THE EXPLODING IMPACT OF IT IN THE DIGITAL ERA

WHY IS THIS IMPORTANT?

We are currently living in the digital era and things are changing exponentially. The first commercial text message was sent in 1992 – today the number sent and received daily exceeds the total population of the planet. In Africa today, more people have a mobile phone than access to safe drinking water. The top 10 in-demand jobs in 2010 did not exist in 2004. We are currently preparing students for jobs that do not yet exist using technologies that have not yet been invented. For students embarking on a four-year technical degree, half of what they learn in their first year will be out of date by their third year of study.

In only a few decades, technology has had a massive impact on both our working and our social lives and will continue to do so at an ever-accelerating rate. We are in the age of unrelenting change that continues to shape our day-to-day lives.

Every one of us will have to learn to live in volatile, uncertain, complex and ambiguous times. As a manager you will have to help your team cope and also, in all probability, show others the way (see Chapter 6 for advice on change leadership).

DELVING A LITTLE DEEPER INTO THE SUBJECT

We are currently living in unique times; times when the younger generation may have more knowledge and know-how than the older generation. Coding is now being taught in primary schools and generation 'Y', for example, has long been predicted to transform traditional communications and media methods to the new wave of social media and smart phone apps. As a new manager it is likely that you are younger than your boss and almost certainly your boss's boss. If this is the case you will have grown up in different times and what appears to be modern technology to your boss or your boss's boss may appear old hat to you.

At the point of transition from technician to manager your technical knowledge and know-how will be up to the minute and at the same time you are in a position of some authority. You are valued and respected – your recent promotion is proof of this. No one within your organisation is in a better place to come up with the ideas that will lead to disruptive innovation, i.e. game changing innovations that create new markets or value propositions.

You are, therefore, ideally placed to have an impact on the strategic direction of your organisation. Use all the skills you have learned in Chapters 9 and 13 to ensure that you are heard and your organisation reaps the benefit of your unique combination of knowledge and capabilities at this transition point in your career.

Be **brave** and be **bold**. Yes you **might** fail, but if you are not brave or bold you certainly **will** fail.

HINTS AND TIPS

Allow yourself a little time each day to think and imagine. Be creative and open your mind to new possibilities. Use the model in Figure 16.1 to focus your thoughts and ideas.

Figure 16.1 Harnessing the potential of IT

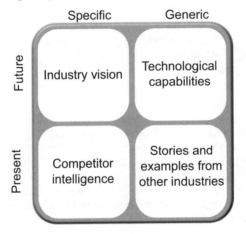

- Think about your competitors – how do they use technology and what do they do differently from you? How could your organisation benefit from adopting some of what they do? What could you do with technology that would place your organisation ahead of the competition?

- Paint a vision of your industry in 5 and 10 years time – what is likely to change and what is likely to remain the same? How will your customers' needs change and how will their interaction with your organisation evolve over time?

- Consider the generic technological capabilities that exist today and those that will exist in the near future; how could you harness them to the advantage of your organisation?

- Consider the stories and examples you read of competitive advantage gained by other industry sectors. What are the common themes? How could any of these be applied to your organisation?

Ask questions, listen carefully and be prepared to challenge the accepted way of doing things. Challenge plans and proposals by asking questions as to why they stop where they do or why your organisation is not aspiring to greater things. Very often you will expose the perceived limitations to be false ones.

Look beyond the ordinary and the obvious and ask questions that reveal possibilities, rather than emphasise limitations. Consider what would happen if you turned a long established policy, rule or belief on its head. For example, consider the *London Evening Standard*; a decade ago it was unthinkable to think of it being free, but in 2009 they did it and improved circulation as a result. They changed the revenue model from one of 'customer pays' to one of advertising revenue.

Think 'off the wall', 'out of the box', weird, wacky, and way out. As Arthur C. Clarke put it so succinctly, 'Any sufficiently advanced technology is indistinguishable from magic' (2000 [1962]).

See Chapter 7 for advice on thinking strategically and Chapter 25 for advice on listening skills.

Use all the skills you have learned in Parts 1 and 2 of this book to build the connections, relationships and trust to get your ideas and suggestions across and ultimately onto the strategic agenda of your organisation. Have the courage and conviction to make your mark.

Any new invention has its downside, and the downside to the digital era is that you will need some knowledge of cyber security and the degree of security appropriate for your organisation. You should have a view as to where the main information risks lie within your organisation and how they are being mitigated. As organisations become more digital, they become more exposed to the danger of cyber-attacks and viruses and the consequences of data loss or outages become more damaging to the organisation.

REFERENCE

Clarke, Arthur C. (2000 [1962]) *Profiles of the future: An inquiry into the limits of the possible*. London: Indigo.

PART 4
THINGS THAT MAY BE KEEPING YOU
AWAKE AT NIGHT

17 MANAGING PEOPLE WHO USED TO BE A PEER, OR WHO ARE OLDER OR MORE EXPERIENCED THAN YOU

WHY IS THIS IMPORTANT?

First you must remember that you were promoted for a reason; you possess some skills, attributes or qualities that your team member or members do not possess. Take pride in that and let it give you confidence. Length of service might have carried weight in the past, but those days have long gone. You are obviously considered to be management material while your ex-peer, older or more experienced team member is not – or at least not yet.

You may have feelings of guilt or be lacking in confidence. Your team member(s) may have feelings of jealousy or resentment.

DELVING A LITTLE DEEPER INTO THE SUBJECT

As a technician, the chances are that you will have been recruited and received positive feedback in relation to your capabilities listed in the two columns on the left of Figure 17.1. You are far more likely, however, to have been promoted in relation to your capabilities listed in the two columns on the right of Figure 17.1.

The skills, qualities and attributes that make you a good technician are very different from those that make you a good manager. In all probability your bosses saw capabilities in you, which relate to the right two columns, that they did not see in the other potential candidate(s) for your job. Look down these two lists and give yourself a score between 10 (I'm great) and 1 (this is something I need to work on). Now consider your ex-peer, older or more experienced team member; how would you score them against the same two lists?

Figure 17.1 People skills, qualities and attributes

Relatively easy to teach	Can teach but difficult	Can't teach but learn by experience	You've either got them or you haven't
Estimating skills Literacy Market/industry awareness Numeracy Planning & organisation Presentation skills Principals of teamwork Report writing Specific & relevant technical capability Work standards	Accuracy Active listening/ questioning Articulateness Coaching & mentoring skills Customer focus Delegation Identifying & respecting difference Impact & influence Motivational techniques Persuasiveness Self awareness Stress handling Tenacity/keeping at it	Anticipation Assertiveness Confidence Courage Cultural awareness Curiosity Decisiveness Empathy Humility Independence Initiative Judgement Leadership Management understanding Managing emotions Organisational understanding Reading people Sociability/mixing Vision	Acceptability/fitting in Career ambition Commitment Creativity/intuition Drive Energy & enthusiasm Flexibility/adaptability Honesty & integrity Intellectual capability Passion Positive 'can do' attitude Resilience Self motivation Sense of humour Team player Technical aptitude Willingness to co-operate Work ethic

HINTS AND TIPS

You can still be friendly and sociable, but you do need to establish your authority. You will do this by gaining their respect and becoming a 'likeable' boss. The art of leadership is getting people to do things for you because they want to, not because they are forced to. Demonstrate the value of the managerial role and your own competence in that role; consider the examples in Chapter 1 (George's story), Chapter 3 (Bob's story) and Chapter 5 (Sarah's story).

Talk to your team, put your cards on the table and agree a way of working together. It is important to clarify things such as what you need from them to make you feel comfortable that they are doing their job well, as well as what they need from you to enable them to do their job to the best of their abilities. Tell them what you value most about them and what you value least. Ask them the same two questions about you. Lay down some ground rules for working together. Ask for their help, and in turn, offer yours.

Take confidence and pride in your promotion to the ranks of management. Do your job to the best of your ability. Do not change your personality from one of friend/team mate to one of an authoritarian dictator. Neither should you be unassertive and let team members ride rough shod over you and get away with inappropriate behaviour or poor performance.

Discover a particular problem or issue that your team has that only a manager would have the authority to resolve, and resolve it for them. Consider the following two mini cases:

Martin was older and more experienced than his manager. He felt he should have been given his manager's job. His boss was an external appointment and Martin was determined to make his life difficult and demonstrate that the company had got it wrong. Martin's new boss talked, asked questions and listened to him; he asked about current projects and the way things worked and got delivered. He found out a little about the culture and key players within the organisation. He also discovered that Martin had a particular issue with the head of IT operations who appeared to be creating unnecessary bureaucracy that negatively impacted implementation schedules. Martin's boss went to talk to the operations manager and listened to his side of the story. They then agreed a compromise solution that involved a fast track process for implementing minor enhancements to existing systems.

This was something that made Martin's life a lot easier and gave his new boss a little credibility in Martin's eyes. Martin then proceeded to test out his new boss by throwing him problems to fix. Martin's new boss rose to the challenge. He fixed those problems that needed to be fixed by a manager such as himself, but he also pushed back when the problems could be resolved by Martin or when the 'problem' was not a problem at all. After a month the 'testing' behaviour ceased and after six months Martin became his boss's most loyal advocate.

John was a friend and peer of Susan; they were both analyst/programmers. Susan got promoted to team leader and became John's boss. John was resentful; he did not really want the job of team leader, but he did not like the fact that his friend was, in his eyes, thought of more highly than himself. Susan tried to reassure him that they could still be friends, but their relationship became tense and distant. Then Susan reflected on an issue that John had confided in her before her promotion took place. John's role required a lot of travel and when he stayed away on business he had to put the travel expenditure on his own credit card and then claim it back at the end of the month. John would frequently exceed his credit limit, which caused difficulty with his personal finances. At his grade John was not entitled to a company credit card. Susan put a case forward and fought the battle for John; she won her case and got him a company credit card. John was eternally grateful and thereafter their friendship was resumed, but with an enhanced degree of respect.

Whatever the situation always remember to keep your cool. See Chapter 25 for advice on conflict resolution.

18 LETTING GO OF THINGS THAT YOU SHOULD NO LONGER BE DOING YOURSELF

WHY IS THIS IMPORTANT?

Making the transition from technician to manager will necessitate becoming less of a 'doer' and more of a coordinator, director, monitor, mentor, broker and facilitator. If you are too busy doing you will not be managing and hence not fulfilling your prime purpose as a manager. Letting go of jobs that you like doing can be difficult and watching others do jobs that you know you can do better and quicker yourself can be very frustrating.

DELVING A LITTLE DEEPER INTO THE SUBJECT

If you have a large team your role will cease to become that of a doer and you will need to become a full-time manager. If you only have a small team you may also need to help in the delivery of tasks for the team. In the latter case your priority should be to develop your staff and help them grow; you should not keep all the juicy or pleasant jobs for yourself. When times are busy you should muck in and do some of the boring, less pleasant tasks. At other times you should do the difficult or potentially contentious tasks and those beyond the current capability of your team members.

HINTS AND TIPS

Letting go of jobs you like doing or that you are good at could be described as 'growing up'. Exercise generosity and take pleasure in watching your staff grow and develop. Perfect the art of delegation, reread all the advice in Chapter 2, and do not forget that you can, and should, be delegating authority, but you can never delegate accountability.

The following story illustrates the difficulties and potential consequences of not being able to let go of cherished jobs.

Some years ago I remember having a secretary who loved booking flights and hotels. In the beginning, when the department was in its infancy, she only had my flights and hotels to book. As the department matured and grew, this activity increased to accommodate about 30 frequent travellers. The flights and hotel booking had become a full-time job, so I recruited an assistant for her. The plan was that the assistant would deal with all the flights and hotel bookings and my secretary could then resume her secretarial duties and support me in my role as European CIO. However, she just could not let go of the flights and hotel booking and, as a consequence, I had an assistant with very little to do and a secretary not performing the duties I needed her to do. Subtle hints turned to direct orders, but all to no avail. Ultimately I had to use shock tactics to motivate her to change her behaviour. I offered a job swap with her assistant along with the consequential change in salary and job title. This did the trick and as a reward I afforded my secretary the luxury of still booking my flights and hotels, but only mine.

You should not be tempted to micro-manage your staff or to let yourself get too involved in their work just because you can. Remember, two people trying to do the same job is a waste of resources and both demoralising and demotivating for the person whose job it should be. Also remember, if you are spending too much time trying to do other people's jobs, you will not be fulfilling your role.

Never ever take a job back if a member of your team is struggling, but develop their competencies by teaching them how to do the job for themselves. This will be time well spent and an investment in the future. See Chapter 28 for advice on coaching skills, and see Chapter 25 for advice on how to manage your own emotions and motivate yourself into doing what you need to do, i.e. let go!

19 COPING WITH STRESS AND PRESSURE

WHY IS THIS IMPORTANT?

Stress and pressure is something that affects all of us from time to time. Stress is now the biggest cause of sickness and absenteeism in the UK, costing the economy billions of pounds a year. It has overtaken backache in the popularity stakes. And to make matters even worse the IT profession is commonly cited as being one of the most stressful professions, often featuring in the top three.

Chronic stress is not good for you and can make you seriously ill. It can contribute to heart disease and memory loss, and it also suppresses the immune response, making you more vulnerable to viral infections and more susceptible to developing certain cancers.

As a new manager you will have your own stresses to cope with and, in addition, you will also need to learn how to deal with those of your team members.

Therefore, you will have to ensure that stress and pressure do not adversely affect you and your ability to do your job. In addition, you have a duty of care to ensure your team members are not put under undue stress and pressure. The following advice will help you recognise the symptoms of stress in both yourself and others, and how to deal with the person or people concerned.

DELVING A LITTLE DEEPER INTO THE SUBJECT

First let us consider the difference between stress and pressure. When under pressure, your body produces adrenaline; this is a positive thing because adrenaline gives you the drive and energy to do things. Without adrenaline coursing around your veins, you may be sorely tempted to stay in bed and have a 'duvet day'. So, pressure enhances your performance, but only up to a certain point. If you exceed your limit and pressure continues to be applied, you will get stressed and your performance will start to decline, as shown in Figure 19.1.

When you are stressed, your body will start to produce a second hormone called cortisol. Cortisol is the hormone designed to keep you safe, to put you in the best physical state to deal with the fight and flight reaction. It was very useful to our ancient ancestors who had the frequent need to fight or flee for their lives. These days, however, few of us have a daily need to fight for our lives or flee from oncoming tigers.

Figure 19.1 Effects of stress on performance

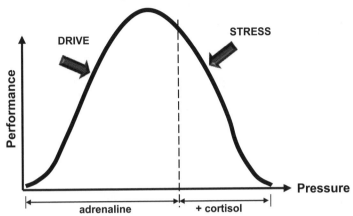

Today, people get stressed in business meetings, by political issues, by people being late, by things we cannot control or not going to plan and by traffic jams, to name but a few. In such situations your body cannot make use of the cortisol rampaging around your blood vessels as it was designed to, i.e. in the form of extreme physical exertion. Instead, the cortisol breaks down into harmful chemicals within your body that may:

- cause damage to the walls of the heart;
- shrink the hippocampus, the part of the brain that turns experiences into memory;
- suppress the immune response, making you more susceptible to picking up bugs and developing cancers.

This is the consequence of living in today's fast and furious, but relatively safe, modern world.

HINTS AND TIPS

Avoiding stress in the first place

First, there are some universal de-stressors, like exercise for example. However, do not be fooled into thinking that this will solve the cortisol problem. Exercise needs to be done at the moment the cortisol is being produced. Going to the gym in the evening after a bad day in the office will do you good generally, but by then the cortisol will have broken down within your body and done its damage.

The only way to resolve the cortisol issue is to either avoid its build-up in the first place or engage in some form of strenuous activity at the moment of its production, such as going for a run around the block or beating the hell out of a punch bag.

Second, go and do something completely different from your day job and something that exercises a different part of your brain. For example, if your job requires a lot of intellectual thought and theorising, try gardening or cooking. If your job involves a lot of human interaction and negotiation, take the dog for a walk or sit down with a good book or crossword puzzle.

Third, read and take heed of the advice in the next chapter on how to achieve a satisfying work/life balance. It may also help to read Chapter 24 on time management.

Finally, take time out to:

- schedule in unscheduled time;
- engage in fun activities;
- engage in relaxing activities;
- pursue hobbies and recreational activities;
- find time for family and friends.

Recognising the signs of stress

The first signs of stress exhibited either by you or by others are likely to be a lack of flexibility and a display of rigidity. Weaknesses may become more pronounced, exaggerated or extreme. People may behave immaturely and could come across as childish, touchy or easily angered. If you can recognise someone when they are just starting to show these symptoms you may be able to help them back to equilibrium by adopting or suggesting some of the tactics in the following section.

Remedies when under stress

It is important to remember that people are different; what may be one person's stressor may be another person's remedy and vice versa. Consider the following list of potential remedies and reflect on what would work for you or the person concerned. If you find it difficult to make a choice now, just try one of the suggestions in the following list and see how it makes you or the person concerned feel. If you or they feel better as a result, carry on; if it is not working, then try something else:

- Talk through your issue with an appropriate person – a close friend or an uninvolved person for example. This can help you to:
  - confront and reframe the problem;
  - receive reassurance or confirmation about a course of action;
  - rebuild self-esteem or confidence to validate competence or worth;
  - receive TLC (tender loving care) from them;
  - decide on priorities or saying no selectively.
- Have some time alone to recover, regroup or regain control.

- Ask for/accept help:

  - in identifying possibilities or options;
  - to share the burden or help with the task.

- Engage in physical activity/exercise.

- Engage in a distracting activity.

- Refocus on the positive – what will work, what can be done – rather than on the negative – what will not work or cannot be done.

Dos and don'ts when dealing with others under stress

When dealing with others under stress it is important to be doubly sensitive. As previously mentioned, people under stress are likely to be touchier, testy and can become easily angered. The following list of dos and don'ts will help avoid any negative reaction to your interventions.

Table 19.1 Dos and don'ts of dealing with others under stress

Do	Do not
• Encourage them to articulate their concerns and try to identify any connections.	• Try to reason with them.
• Actively listen to what they are telling you without interruption or judgement.	• Contradict them.
• Acknowledge their feelings and empathise with them.	• Tell them what to do.
• Ask them what it is about certain situations that make them particularly stressful. Try to identify the triggers.	• Minimise or dismiss the concerns they have expressed.
• Ask them what would need to change for them not to feel this way if and when that trigger event happens again.	• Make fun of anything.
• Get them to talk through their feelings and, in doing so, to identify a way forward.	• Apply even more pressure.
• Offer to support them in any appropriate and practical way. This may involve offering to refer them to staff welfare, HR or for external counselling, for example.	• Tell them that you know exactly how they feel.
	• Tell them it will be 'OK'.

20 ACHIEVING A SATISFYING WORK/LIFE BALANCE

WHY IS THIS IMPORTANT?

Read any newspaper or magazine and you will see that work/life balance is fast becoming the hot career issue of the decade. Do you read and respond to emails at home in the evenings or at weekends? What about holidays – do you switch off and relax or do you keep in touch with the office?

When I started work at a shipyard in the early 1980s, email and mobile phones did not exist. When you left work, you left work. When you went on holiday, you went on holiday. In those days the entire shipyard closed for a fortnight. Therefore, on your return from holiday you just picked things back up as you had left them two weeks previously; no last-minute rush before you departed or frantic catch-up on your return.

Today life is very different. With the advent of modern technology, we literally have the ability to work any time, any place and anywhere. Today even air travel is no longer a barrier to your ability to keep in contact with the rest of the world. What is it about the nature of our organisations and our society that make us so reluctant to be out of contact, to let go and have any 'me' time? What is it about our bosses and other key stakeholders that expect us to be 'always available' and never off duty? And is the IT profession leading the way?

DELVING A LITTLE DEEPER INTO THE SUBJECT

I recently discovered a new word in a psychology magazine, 'weisure', used to describe the time you spend when you are not at work but you are still working. Activities that fall into this category include reading your email rather than a newspaper or a novel on your train journey home from work, or talking about that afternoon's meeting at after-work drinks.

If you want evidence of this phenomenon, look no further that the annual email-addiction survey run by AOL. Some of the results are truly startling and, perhaps worryingly, most of us will probably confess to having done at least some of these things ourselves at some time:

- 62% of people check work emails at weekends.
- 59% of people check email from the bathroom.
- 19% of people choose vacation spots with access to email.

Indeed, *ITV Tonight* recently commissioned a survey asking 2,000 full-time employees about their working lives. The results revealed a nation feeling the pressure of juggling work and home:

- 70% said they were spending most of their lives working.
- More than 50% said they worked more hours than they were paid for.
- 32% felt that working too hard had made them ill.
- 74% believed that they suffered work-related stress.
- One in five admitted to spending only 20 minutes a day with their children.

We are all guilty of this gradual drift towards a reluctance, or inability, to switch off from work. It might seem like a good use of 'dead time' but too much 'weisure' time means you do not switch off enough, which is bad for your mind and your body. Consider the following statement:

In early life, people give up their health to gain wealth. Then in later life, they give up wealth to regain their health.

Now genuinely answer the following question: Do you work to live or live to work?

Most of the literature in relation to work/life balance advises you to improve your time management, become better at prioritising and delegating, turn off new email alerts and tackle them in focused bouts – in essence, to work smarter rather than harder. I believe that solving issues around work/life balance has to go deeper than simply getting better at time management.

Better time management on its own simply helps you to do more of the same, to be more focused and effective on a particular aspect of your life. Adjustments to work/life balance require a change in attitude and priorities and a shift of mindset.

Consider Maslow's classic hierarchy of needs, developed in the 1940s, in Figure 20.1.

How much of your time and mental energies are focused at the pinnacle of Maslow's hierarchy of needs, on 'fulfilment'? Could you readily articulate your life's purpose if asked to?

Does modern society and the work ethic of today encourage you to focus more of your effort on certain levels of the hierarchy and less on others?

In today's world, survival and security are inextricably linked by the psychological pressure to acquire and maintain a certain lifestyle. Although Western society will ensure that few people are likely to starve to death, the psychological pressures to ensure your future security are probably greater than those encountered by the previous generation. You can no longer expect the luxury of a job for life or an index-linked pension.

With the advent of LinkedIn, Facebook, Twitter, blogs, wikis and so on, you are encouraged to belong to, interact with and contribute to society as a whole; not just the people you interact with on a daily basis, but potentially the whole world. Your presence is

Figure 20.1 Maslow's hierarchy of needs

global, along with your reputation and the opportunity for international prestige and recognition. Does the modern world encourage you to trade more survival, security and esteem for less belonging, affection and fulfilment?

Human beings are social creatures. Therefore, it is important for you to feel a sense of belonging and acceptance, to give and receive love and affection. In the absence of these, you become susceptible to loneliness, social anxiety and, ultimately, clinical depression.

A sense of belonging may be fulfilled by club membership, the office environment, professional organisations, sports teams, religious groups, social connections with friends, family members or close colleagues, to name but a few. A sense of belonging is not, however, achieved on the Internet; it requires both physical presence and emotional connection. Technology and modern society encourage you to spend less and less time interacting with people face to face.

Scientists will warn you that this is at your peril. Studies into brain chemistry have demonstrated that positive human-to-human contact affects your hormone balance; it increases the levels of helpful hormones that make you feel good and promote trust and bonding, and reduces the level of stress hormones that ultimately make you ill.

Consider the adaptation of the classic project management triangle in Figure 20.2. You need to work out how to live your life, given the constraint of only 24 hours in any one day. There are three key factors that you need to address and juggle in relation to your work/life balance; spending less time on one will allow more time and flexibility in the other two areas. Spending more time on one area will afford you less time and flexibility in the other two areas and this is when you should consciously consider the consequences. During an 'Ideal' working day, you may spend approximately eight hours on personal care, eight hours on leisure and eight hours working. If you spend more time working, you spend less time on leisure and/or personal care. The consequence is likely

Figure 20.2 Work/life balance triangle

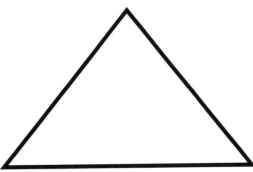

Working, travelling from and to

Leisure i.e. socialising with friends and family, sports, hobbies, games, watching TV, etc

Personal care i.e. eating, sleeping, washing, etc

to be exhaustion, both physically and mentally. In the long term, your health, well-being and personal relationships are liable to suffer.

According to the Organisation for Economic Co-operation and Development (OECD), the Danes top the bill for the country with the best work/life balance. Their findings revealed that Danes devote 68 per cent of their day, i.e. 16.3 hours, to personal care and leisure, the ideal mix! Only 0.02 per cent of Danes work more than 50 hours a week. Also, 78 per cent of Danish mothers go back to work once their children are in school. In the study, the UK failed to feature anywhere in the top 10.

In the same vein, a UK study by the Institute of Leadership and Management found that two in five managers did not take their full holiday entitlement during 2013. That is a whopping 40 per cent!

HINTS AND TIPS

The top level of Maslow's hierarchy of needs symbolises a state of being in which the highest levels of fulfilment and individual happiness are achieved. For each individual this will be different. One person, for example, may have a strong desire to become an ideal parent; another may wish to be a top athlete; while a third may find fulfilment in painting and the arts. We may also take pleasure and find fulfilment from helping others or in silence and tranquillity, for example.

What is your 'life purpose'? What would make you look back in your old age and say 'I have had a happy and fulfilling life with no regrets'? The following exercise will help you articulate your life purpose and what happiness and fulfilment would mean for you. You will find a list of personal values in Table 20.1.

Personal values are deeply held views of what we, as individuals, find worthwhile and meaningful in our lives. Sometimes they are coded into our brains at such a fundamental level that we are unable to see them easily. For many of us, they are rarely brought to the surface and questioned and it is for this reason that they can create inner conflict. Without awareness of our fundamental values, it is difficult for us to ensure fulfilment in our lives.

Step one: 'What do I value most?' From the list of values (both work and personal), select the 10 that are the most important to you – as guides for how to behave or as components of a valued way of life. If you feel any are missing, add those values of your own to the list.

Table 20.1 List of values

Things you value most

advancement and promotion	fortune and material wealth	power and authority
adventure	fun	privacy
arts	having a family	public service
being home	having a 'soulmate'	public recognition
beating my personal best	helping other people	quality in what i do
'can do' attitude; finding a way	helping society	religion
challenging complex problems	honesty and integrity	recognition from those i care about
change and variety	independence	reputation
competence	influencing others	respect for others
competition	inner harmony	responsibility and accountability
creativity	innovation	search for truth
decisiveness	intellectual status	security
dependable	job tranquillity	self-achievement
ecological awareness	knowledge	self-respect
economic security	leadership	sharing affection with others
effectiveness	love of country	simplicity

(Continued)

Table 20.1 (Continued)

Things you value most

efficiency	loyalty	stability
ethical practice	meaningful work	status
excellence	membership of the community	team work
excitement	money	telling the truth
fame	openness and being straightforward	tolerance
fast living	order (tranquillity, stability, conformity)	transparency
fast-paced work	personal challenge	trust
freedom	personal growth and development	wisdom
friendship	physical challenge	work under pressure

Step two: 'From 10 to 3' – having identified 10 values, imagine you are only permitted to have 5:

- Cross out the five you would give up.
- Now cross out one or more so that you are down to four values.
- And finally cross out another to bring you down to three values.

Now you have the three values you care most about.

Step three: 'Articulation' – take a look at these three values:

- What specifically do they mean for you? What do you expect from yourself as a result of these values – even in bad times?
- How would your life be different if those values were even more prominent and practised?
- What would an organisation be like that encouraged employees to live up to your values? Does your life (both working and private) permit you to 'live out' your values and gain happiness and fulfilment? Use the work/life balance triangle (Figure 20.2) to help you with this one – how much time do you spend at each point of the triangle?

- Where are your core values exercised/fulfilled? Does this split work for you?
- Is any aspect suffering at the expense of the others? What gives when the pressure is on?

Step four: 'Rebalancing' – assuming this split does not work for you (or why else would you be reading this chapter?), you need to make changes in your life. This will require a mindset shift otherwise your plans will remain mere good intentions that never come to fruition. Also, remember work and other jobs, such as DIY, have a tendency to expand to fill the time available.

Here are a few examples of things you might consider doing:

- Sleep – make sure you get enough; most of us need around seven to eight hours per night. Without a good night's sleep you will not function either efficiently or effectively. Tasks will take twice as long as they should do and the results will be substandard.
- Exercise – make sure you get a little every day, even if it is taking the stairs rather than the lift.
- Eat properly – we cannot function without fuel, so make sure you get a well-balanced diet, avoid sugary foods and eat your greens.
- Get some 'me' time – everyone needs a little 'me' time each day to recharge those emotional batteries. Read a fiction book or newspaper on that plane or train journey rather than doing that report or checking your email.
- Get some leisure/family time – leave your briefcase in the office apart from those exceptional circumstances. Switch off your work phone in the evenings and at weekends – if it is really urgent they will phone you on your personal number.
- Spend quality time with your family – arrange to do things, go for a walk in the park, visit friends, etc.
- Model yourself on the Danes – restrict your working hours to no more than 40 hours per week. You will be surprised at how much more effective you will be when you are fresh, relaxed and energised. If you work in the type of organisation that values physical presence over output, do not follow the herd; instead become a role model for others. Work fewer hours than the norm, but, within those hours, make a truly significant and high-quality contribution that gets you noticed. Ultimately you will find that by spending more quality time with your family, by injecting slack into your schedule and allowing yourself 'me' time, you will have more energy to be super-inspirational and super-productive when you are at work.

21 MANAGING AND ENHANCING YOUR REPUTATION

WHY IS THIS IMPORTANT?

Perception is everything – it is not what you are but what others perceive you to be that is important. What they see first is your reputation – this is the cumulative effect of all your deeds and how others perceive and interpret those deeds. It will also be coloured by the stereotypical images held about the professional and social groups to which you belong.

Reputation tends to precede people, and others will form opinions about you before they have even met you. They will have already formed an impression of what you may be like based upon their stereotypical image of people in your profession or from your walk of life and/or from what they have heard about you from others. When they do meet you, they will at first pick up on any indicators that reinforce their predetermined view; they will pay less attention to any counter indications.

Most people leave their reputation to chance; they do not actively try to manage the impressions that they create. For others the situation is even worse – they go unnoticed in organisations because they are buried deep within their specialist departments and nobody, especially themselves, is working proactively to advertise their talents to a wider audience. It is not enough to be good; you have to be seen to be good! It is only then that you will get the recognition that you deserve.

DELVING A LITTLE DEEPER INTO THE SUBJECT

Just as people tend to classify problems, opportunities and other business phenomena, they classify others. It is a type of shorthand for making sense of the world.

From an evolutionary point of view, there is enormous survival value in an ability to make rapid judgements about people and situations. Imagine those days when people were walking the Savannah plains and bumping into other living creatures; they had to make fairly instant decisions about whether these were friend or foe – people's lives depended upon it. Analysing options and next steps was not a recipe for a long and fruitful life. Even today, despite years of education, development and sensitisation to political correctness, the sorting of people into 'in-groups' and 'out-groups' remains one of the primary ways of evaluating others. This is why first impressions are so important.

Human brains work with clusters of concepts, often referred to as 'neuronal groups'. Rather than building impressions of the world by adding up the individual pieces of data, people make 'intuitive leaps'. Their brains are capable of jumping to conclusions because limited data is quickly matched against a number of 'templates' in the brain. So people's natural tendency is not to say (unconsciously), 'This person or thing will remain unclassified until I have acquired enough evidence', it is to say (unconsciously), 'What predefined pattern most closely matches my initial impression?' This instant classification remains current until enough contrary evidence forces them to reclassify. More often than not, the effort of reclassification is too difficult and, despite evidence to the contrary, people stick with their initial assessment.

When people do not know you, or meet you for the first time, the default assumption, if you are associated with the world of IT, is likely to be the IT stereotype. Unless you take responsibility for making yourself visible and managing your own reputation, you will wake up one morning to find that you have a reputation that is solely based on a stereotypical view and the impressions and imaginings of others.

Managing your reputation is not about bragging about how great you are; rather, it is about sending out the right messages and endeavouring to be what you desire to appear. Think about how you would like people to introduce you or refer to you. For example, when your CEO asks a colleague who you are, you do not want that colleague merely to say, 'Oh that is Peter from IT' or 'That is Jane who looks after the help desk'. You need to stand out from the crowd, to be unique, to be more than your role. This means the sort of response you are aiming for is something along the lines of, 'Oh that is Peter, he's your man if you have a failing project that needs turning around' or 'That is Jane, she's a wiz at winning over difficult customers'. The key to developing a good reputation is to let others do the work for you. You need to build a network of personal advocates – people who will spontaneously sing your praises and reinforce your 'brand' image.

Never forget that it can take years to build a good reputation, but only seconds to destroy it.

HINTS AND TIPS

First impressions

You cannot change the IT stereotype, but you can change what your own peers and colleagues think of you as an individual – provided, of course, that they get to know you as an individual. This is another reason why networking is so important.

I have been researching the IT stereotype for the past decade and over that period I have seen little change. Its key characteristics are someone who:

- is comfortable with logic, facts and data, but ...;
- is uncomfortable with ambiguity and unpredictability – they like to follow clear and unambiguous rules;

- lives in a world of black and white where there are no shades of grey – there is a right way to build a system and a wrong way to build a system;

- is politically naïve and lacking in business awareness;

- is cautious, conservative and risk-averse;

- is good at deconstructing problems, but poor at synthesis, i.e. understanding in the context of the greater whole;

- lacks interpersonal skills and a sense of humour;

- adopts a victim mentality – cannot win, so will not fight;

- is poor at accepting criticism – often rationalising it away.

Stereotypical images take a long time to change, particularly when they are reinforced by the media and repeated showings of the *IT Crowd*, for example. Your job is to confront the image, to behave anti-stereotypically and to talk openly about it. Here are a few suggestions:

- Discuss openly the traits, habits, routines, rituals, stories, myths, symbols, style, dress code and so on that are associated with your profession. Articulating concerns, barriers and oddities makes them less powerful.

- Talk 'big picture', have a view about business matters in general, demonstrate a forward-thinking 'can do' attitude and that you have a sense of humour.

- Emulate how the business people within your organisation dress rather than how the stereotypical IT person dresses. Talk business jargon rather than technical jargon. Do not do anything that might reinforce the IT stereotype – unlike one IT director I knew who still carried his screwdriver around in his top pocket!

- Stop focusing on metrics and benchmarks and start focusing on building relationships, trust and adding value.

- Do not overanalyse situations; apply the 80:20 rule (see Chapter 24 on time management for more details).

- Talk about your organisation as a whole and where your industry is going rather than your functional discipline.

- Stop focusing on the nuts and bolts of current issues and start focusing on innovation and future directions.

- Stop talking about problems and start talking about possibilities.

- Be likeable – someone that others want to spend time with:

  - Be warm and friendly; keep smiling.

  - Always speak well of others; look for opportunities to say thank you or well done.

  - Keep an open mind and be tolerant of others – reserve judgement and accept their values and beliefs.

- Be open and honest, flexible and collaborative, patient and understanding.
- Ask open, gentle, encouraging questions of inquiry – be prepared to listen and learn.
- Share a little of yourself to encourage others to open up.
- Keep your cool and use humour to diffuse tension or get difficult messages across.
- Stop taking yourself too seriously, learn to laugh at yourself.
- Do not be touchy, prissy, precious or easily offended.

Developing a personal 'brand'

Sit down with a pen and paper and think about your 'brand' image:

- What would you like to be known for?
- What are you really good at?
- What have your prime contributions been?
- How have you added value?
- What is your biggest achievement to date?
- What words and phrases would you use to describe yourself?
- What words and phrases would others use to describe you as a person?

Now structure these thoughts under four headings, as in Figure 21.1:

- Your values – what you stand for, e.g. honesty, fairness, commitment to sustainability and so on.
- The reason to believe in you – these will include personal testimonials, expert endorsements, awards and professional achievements, case studies or demonstrations of what you can do.
- The benefits of working with you – why someone would choose you over someone else? This is likely to reflect your most visible talent or skill, e.g. because you are a great communicator or because you are a Six Sigma black belt.
- What makes you unique – what sets you apart from the crowd? What have you achieved that no one else in your organisation has? What is different about you? What unusual experiences have you had?

Finally, think about the words and phrases that you would like to spring to mind spontaneously when other people think or talk about you; for example, a problem solver, an ideas person or a team player. You will note that these examples are all outwardly focused, they speak about what a person could bring to the party to help their organisation and they are a promise to deliver. A personal brand is very similar to that of a product brand; you may deliver the promise of 'trustworthiness', for example, in the same way that Apple may deliver the promise of 'cool to own' or Volvo the promise of 'safety'.

Figure 21.1 Your personal brand

Once you have understood what you are about, i.e. your brand, you need to start living that brand:

- Make sure that all your words and deeds are consistent and congruent with your brand – everyone you touch needs to receive the same message and see the same person.

- Keep your message simple, unambiguous and easy to interpret.

- Focus on outcomes, i.e. the capacity you have to make a difference to other people's lives, what you can help people or your organisation to achieve.

- Be visible – you cannot achieve effective personal branding by hiding behind your role or staying in your box. I will talk more about this in the next section on networking.

- Be heard – once you are out and being seen, you also have to make sure that you are heard. Remember that what you say is only 10 per cent of the equation – the other 90 per cent is how you say it, how your actions are in congruence with what you say and how you follow through on your words and actions.

Networking

You should take advantage of any and every opportunity that presents itself to network and commence the process of relationship building. When I talk about networking I am not talking about connecting with people on LinkedIn or Facebook. While they are useful tools in many ways, you cannot build a trust-based relationship by simply connecting with someone on a social media site. You can become inquisitive about someone, you can even develop the beginnings of a sense of liking, but trust can only be built through face-to-face interaction over a significant period of time.

So, when I talk of networking I mean a purposeful social interaction that builds a trusting relationship and results in someone being willing to risk their own reputation by recommending you. In so doing you will develop an army of allies and advocates who will work to develop your reputation for you.

Some of your networking efforts will be opportunistic; others will be planned. When you go to a conference, for example, forget your phone and your email and focus your attention on the people physically there. For that day, and that day only, you have the opportunity to meet with them face to face and start a relationship. In all likelihood this is an opportunity never to be repeated.

As far as planned networking is concerned, you are unlikely to have the time to get to know everyone that you could possibly meet, so you need to establish a strategy on how to target and prioritise your networking efforts. I suggest that you work on the following groups in the following order:

- Inside your organisation: make it your business to find out who the key players are in each department, who is sponsoring each major IT project or programme, who is managing each project on behalf of the sponsor and who reports directly to board members. These are all people who should be in your circle of influence.

- Outside your organisation, but inside your professional discipline: you already have something in common – your area of expertise. Look for opportunities to engage with people in communities such as:

  - Your customer community – the people who use and care about the goods and services that you provide.

  - Specialist groups under the banner of your professional body.

  - If you are in the private sector, journalists (both retained and freelance) who write on your subject.

  - Conference organisers and speakers.

- Outside your professional discipline, but working in the same sector as you: this is playing the long game but it does have two big advantages:

  - It helps you understand the needs and drivers of people who face different problems from yours and gives you valuable practice at building relationships where you do not have a common bond of professional knowledge.

  - It can give you new insights that you would never pick up by interacting with like-minded people – this sort of boundary spanning is often where innovative ideas are born; it also makes you a key asset on cross-functional teams.

So, now you have narrowed down the universe to a handful of 15 to 25 people that you will target in order to expand your circle of influence. You now need to make opportunities to interact with these people, find out what you can do for them and show them that they can rely upon you. You may, for example, be able to help them solve a problem, facilitate access to a resource that is unavailable to them or introduce them to like-minded people. Make full use of your relationship management skills (Chapter 14), your communication skills (Chapter 8) and your influencing skills (Chapter 9).

22 HOW TO DEAL WITH ORGANISATIONAL POLITICS

WHY IS THIS IMPORTANT?

In the workplace organisational politics are a fact of life. Organisations, being made up of people, are essentially political institutions. All business professionals need to be adept at dealing with political situations, but some are better at it than others.

Unfortunately, there is no single formula for success. Politics are often messy, ambiguous and unpredictable; and to top it all, being right is not enough. Outcomes in the political arena depend upon the subtle interactions and interplays between people. Each situation will be different and unique and what proves successful in one situation may prove disastrous in the next. In essence, organisational politics is an art rather than a science!

Organisational politics are often construed as being destructive, time-wasting or unethical. Ask anyone what words and phrases spring to mind when you mention the words 'organisational politics' and 9 times out of 10 you will get responses such as:

- doing deals;
- scoring points;
- personal agendas;
- getting one over on one's colleagues;
- secrecy and subterfuge;
- Mafiosi tactics;
- win–lose situations.

Organisational politics are, however, simply the result of differing opinions, values, standpoints, perceptions and so on. As such, they can be dealt with either positively or negatively. On the positive side, organisational politics are about:

- influence;
- collaboration;
- building relationships;
- openness and honesty;

113

- being streetwise;
- win–win situations.

Participating in organisational politics is not an option, but how you choose to participate is. The choice is yours, either positively or negatively, and the outcomes are of your own making.

DELVING A LITTLE DEEPER INTO THE SUBJECT

Researchers, Baddeley and James, studied leaders who had attained long-term political success within their organisations. They attributed their success to the following two key dimensions:

1. Acting from an informed and knowledgeable position that demonstrates:

   - an understanding of the decision-making processes within their organisation;
   - an awareness of both the overt and covert agendas of the key decision makers;
   - an innate understanding of who has the power within the organisation and what gives one power;
   - a willingness to go above that extra mile to help others even if it is not part of their job description;
   - an understanding of the style and culture of the organisation;
   - a sense of the meaning of 'politics' in the context of their organisation.

2. Acting with integrity as defined by the following principles:

   - avoiding playing psychological games with people;
   - accepting themselves and others for what they are – human beings who all have their associated strengths, weaknesses and imperfections;
   - seeking to find win–win strategies in difficult/conflicting situations.

Figure 22.1 utilises these two dimensions and is adapted from the work of Baddeley and James. Each quadrant of the model is illustrated with an animal analogy to create a political zoo. The **innocent sheep** acts with integrity, but has no clue about what is going on in the organisational sense. The **clever fox** knows exactly what is going on, but uses this knowledge to exploit the weaknesses of others. The **inept baboon** neither acts with integrity nor knows what is going on. The **wise dolphin** possesses both understanding and integrity and hence represents my icon of political success.

Figure 22.1 The political zoo

The behaviour of the four animals is described below in greater detail:

Sheep see the world through simplistic eyes; they believe you are right if you are in a position of authority. They do what they are told, stick to the rules, are too busy to network and do not know how to build coalitions and alliances. They act with integrity but are street naïve.

Foxes know exactly what is going on, but use this knowledge to exploit the weaknesses in others. They are self-centred, but with a charming veneer. They are manipulative and like games involving winners and losers; and they love leading lambs to the slaughterhouse.

Baboons are not tuned in to the grapevine; their antennae are blocked, and they therefore end up conspiring with the powerless. They are emotionally illiterate, seeing things in black and white and not recognising when they are fighting a losing battle. They play games with people but do not understand why they keep losing.

Dolphins take account of other people personally; they are excellent listeners and aware of others' viewpoints. They are non-defensive, open and share information. They use creativity and imagination to engineer win–win situations. They act from both an informed and an ethical standpoint; they are both streetwise and virtuous.

What characterises the dolphin is calmness in a storm, a certainty about their own destiny and a thirst to learn from others. They may be busy, but not stressed or pressured; and they can always find the time to work alongside colleagues or help others out. People have respect for them as model human beings first and their competence in their professional capacity second.

HINTS AND TIPS

People will behave as each of the four animals from time to time; however, it is about one's prime behaviour. The aim of this book is to help you move to the top of the model, left or right is, however, your choice, I hope your aim would be to become a 'dolphin'. Here are a few examples of how the four animals would behave in various situations:

- **When in situations of conflict the**

  - **Dolphin** asks, 'how can we work together to solve this one?'
  - **Fox** asserts, 'I am not prepared to change my position.'
  - **Baboon** declares, 'I can't agree and would prefer not to discuss it anyway.'
  - **Sheep** mutters, 'I concede the point and will accept whatever you say.'

- **When responding to or giving orders the**

  - **Dolphin** looks for opportunities to go beyond the call of duty, to extend their sphere of influence and to develop the potential in others.
  - **Fox** demands, 'do as you are told – it's my way or the highway.'
  - **Baboon** bleats, 'that's outside my brief – I won't do it.'
  - **Sheep** says meekly, 'I will do as you say.'

- **When communicating with others the**

  - **Dolphin** actively listens, is open and shares information.
  - **Fox** is dismissive of alternative view points, looks for a fight and believes that information is power.
  - **Baboon** whinges and moans to others who are equally powerless.
  - **Sheep** keeps its head down and keeps quiet about anything potentially controversial.

- **When considering the phrase 'organisational politics' the**

  - **Dolphin** believes that organisational politics are a fact of life and are about influence, collaboration and achieving win–win.
  - **Fox** believes that organisational politics is a sport; it is about winners and losers and about coming out on top – it involves manipulation and exploitation to achieve one's own ends.

- **Baboon** believes that organisational politics is a game, but it does not understand why it keeps losing.

- **Sheep** believes that it does not enter into the game of organisational politics – it is just everyone else!

Considering your own behaviour today within your current role: which of the political 'animals' best represents you and which do you aspire to become? If 'dolphinism' is your aim, the five single most important things you can do are as follows:

1. **Develop your network** – build positive relationships with everyone and anyone; create allies and advocates and build coalitions and alliances (see Chapters 14 and 21 for more details). Use your network to find out what is going on, to learn, to acquire those nuggets of wisdom and to tap into the organisational grapevine.

2. **Be someone that can be trusted** – always do what you will say you will do, never give people false hopes. Do not give empty promises because it is the easiest thing to do, and genuinely mean what you say. Remember, when it comes to trust, actions speak louder than words.

3. **Be generous** – give a little of yourself to others, whether that is your time, your expertise, your knowledge, your help or your support, without expecting anything in return. Look for the good in others, assume they have good intentions and stay curious to find out what these are even when they are not obvious or the person is behaving negatively. Be prepared to forgive and offer people a face-saving route if they need to change their minds or behave differently.

4. **Listen and learn** – actively listen to others, focus on what they are saying rather than thinking about what you are going to say next. Accept what they say without judgement or criticism, try to put yourself in their shoes and view the situation from their perspective – you may learn something that surprises you. Remember that perception is reality in the eye of the beholder.

5. **Look for the win–win** – if you want somebody to do something for you, always consider why they should do it; the 'what's in it for them?' question. Think about why you do things that others have asked of you, or why you do not, as the case may be. It may be because you like the person, because it is an interesting task or because it will enhance your skills or reputation. It could be to gain 'brownie' points, because you owe someone, to build trust and, of course, many, many more reasons. People are far more likely to do something that you want them to do if there is something in it for them. Learn people's motivators and tap into them; this way you will engage both heart and mind.

Dealing with the foxes of the world

Foxes are self-centred, and senior ones are also invariably egotistical while the more junior ones may be narcissistic. Your tactics for handling such individuals may include:

- Make them feel good about themselves:

  - Help them to develop their skills and to shine at something.

  - Build on their suggestions – use the words 'yes and ...' to steer them rather than 'yes, but ...'.

  - Help them to think through the consequences of their actions by using the questioning techniques described in Chapter 28.

  - Offer them the 'limelight'.

  - Massage their ego and praise their intellect.

  - Get them to talk about themselves – remember, this is most people's favourite subject. This will have the added benefit of getting to know your 'enemy'.

- Make them feel comfortable about you:

  - Help them to understand you – your values and drivers.

  - Be truthful and transparent.

- Do not give them any ammunition:

  - Be firm and strong.

  - Do not be sloppy or slapdash.

  - Keep your cool.

- Protect yourself:

  - Cultivate your friends – there is safety in numbers.

  - Cultivate allies – this will limit the bully's sphere of influence.

  - Keep positive about yourself and maintain your values.

The following mini case illustrates how a relatively junior IT manager successfully dealt with a fox and prevented a flawed change initiative from having a detrimental impact on the organisation in question.

A medium-sized financial services company was predicting substantial growth. As a consequence they needed to update their ancient sales and marketing system. As time was of the essence, IT chose a package solution. The only downside with their choice was that the sales and marketing system was heavily integrated into the vendor's own CRM system; taking the sales and marketing system meant taking the CRM system as well. This was likely to meet with some resistance from their business customers, who were not asking for any change to their existing CRM system. The existing one was familiar to them, liked and it did the job. The CIO's view was that the business customers were lacking in vision about the future, and too set in their ways for the good of the company.

The board gave its approval and the project got underway. In the event, the development costs for the modifications to the system grew significantly. There were far more difficulties than either the company or the vendors had anticipated in getting the system to work within the business. There were an almost unending series of 'complications'; no one was deliberately trying to sabotage the system, but it seemed that, day by day, new problems arose.

Time was now passing. The anticipated growth in business had not happened, so the initial need for a new system had receded. But the CIO had already exceeded budget, the current investment totalling some £15 million to date, and considerable work had been done on modifying the CRM element of the new system to fulfil the business needs. The CIO had a difficult decision to make. His choices were:

1. To carry on with the whole project, incurring, inevitably, further and unpredictable costs.
2. A compromise solution whereby the company tried to salvage something from the project, such as the new CRM system, which was the only part of the project that looked viable. However, there was still the problem that the business saw no need for, and did not want, a new CRM system.
3. To abandon the whole project and write the money off to experience.
4. To try to offset some of the blame onto the software supplier.

The CIO in the case was a foxy character with an eye to promotion. His first reaction was to take option 4. However, this was soon discounted on the advice of the lawyers and the cost of litigation. Therefore, option 2 became the CIO's favoured route forward.

However, a relatively junior manager involved in the project challenged the CIO's rational. He followed the CIO to the coffee machine one day and started asking questions about the project; general ones to start, e.g. 'how do you feel the project is going?', and then more specific questions such as 'can you talk me through the business case?', 'how much resistance do you perceive from the banking director?' (who was a powerful antagonist) and 'if we were starting with a blank sheet of paper, would we be embarking on this project today?'.

By asking such questions, he helped the CIO to think through the consequences of his actions, i.e. that sunk cost was not a justification for going forward and was akin to throwing good money after bad, that there was no business case for moving forward and that the likely consequence would be damaged relationships with the business and hence lack of trust in IT. All these factors would ultimately have a negative impact on the CIO's own reputation.

Again through questioning, he then helped the CIO to come up with an alternative solution that was both a win for the company and a win for the CIO. They packaged up the new CRM for sale elsewhere within the group – the Hong Kong office got something they desperately needed, the UK business was not forced to have something it did not want and the UK IT department became a profit centre. All these factors enhanced the reputation of the CIO.

23 MY BOSS IS A BULLY – HOW DO I COPE?

WHY IS THIS IMPORTANT?

If it is happening to you, you are not alone. Bullying is common within IT; a recent study by IDG Connect revealed that 75 per cent of IT professionals surveyed claimed to have been bullied at work, while 85 per cent said they had seen others bullied. The IT stereotype is characterised as someone who has a high intellect, but is lacking in people skills or emotional intelligence (see Chapter 25 for more on emotional intelligence, or EQ for short); both bullies and victims are lacking in EQ.

If you feel bullied then this is an issue and you should not let others belittle or make light of your feelings. However, you also need to look at the situation from your boss's perspective and through their value and belief systems. Their behaviour may stem from frustration rather than malice. For example, some managers believe that if you are not aiming to progress up through the ranks of an organisation, you have given up and are on a slippery slope of decline. You, on the other hand, may be the type of person who is happy where they are and not pushing for promotion to the next level. The perceived bulling behaviour of your boss may therefore be borne out of frustration that you are not achieving what your boss feels you are capable of.

Remember that although the problem may lie with your boss, the bully, the solution is in your hands.

DELVING A LITTLE DEEPER INTO THE SUBJECT

Bullying is incredibly destructive; it leaves a person feeling powerless, confused, upset, angry and exhausted. It can destroy your self-esteem and totally undermine your ability to achieve anything positive. Productivity and self-confidence suffer, which impact both the individual and the organisation alike.

Just because you feel bullied or perceive your boss to be a bully, it does not necessarily mean that this is either your boss's intent or that they are inherently a bad person. Your boss may be suffering from frustration, lack of self-esteem, abuse, ineptitude or such-like. A clash of styles or value systems can also result in the perception of being bullied.

Malevolent intent is a core component of deep-seated bullying. This intent may be conscious or unconscious. Genuine bullies can be extremely destructive, but are fortunately quite rare. In order to help you deal with them, it may help to categorise them according to their degree of cleverness and also their degree of self-control, as illustrated in Figure 23.1.

Figure 23.1 Types of bully

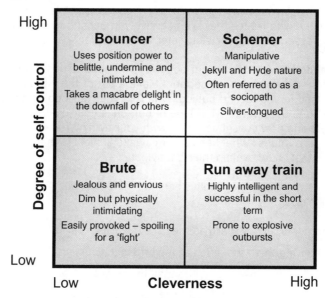

Let us explore the four types in a little greater depth.

The brutes – these are the easiest to spot. Their lack of self-control means that they are prone to sudden and uncontrolled outbursts, which can be physically intimidating. Because they are not too clever, they do not think through the consequences of their actions for others or indeed for themselves.

The bouncers – in some ways these are like brutes, but either through training or because of their position, they have learned to control their emotions. However, under stress they still tend to rely on physical or emotional pressure to get their own way. They are seldom overtly aggressive, but they know how to apply pressure and they can be relentless in doing so in order to get what they want.

The runaway trains – these people are clever so they know how to manipulate people in order to get what they want. However, their lack of self-control means that they are totally unpredictable and their attention is likely to wander. These are difficult bullies to deal with, as you can never be quite clear about what might tip them over the edge.

The schemers – these are the most dangerous of all and also the most difficult type of bully to deal with. They are both clever and in control and therefore extremely difficult to expose. They are silver-tongued and most people would view them as wonderful people. The 'Hyde' side of their character would only be revealed to an unfortunate few. Bullies in this category are commonly referred to as 'sociopaths'.

HINTS AND TIPS

The first step is to determine whether malice is intended or not. Is your boss a true bully or simply someone with issues that are negatively impacting their behaviour towards you? Once you have made this decision, refer to the relevant category as follows.

No malice intended – with this type of boss you will need to understand why you feel bullied – the root cause of this perception. Make a list of the situations and circumstances that result in you feeling bullied. What did your boss do or not do, say or not say? What led up to this event? What type of person is your boss? What is their communication style and how does it compare with your own? What is important to them? What are their core values? What keeps them awake at night? What pressures are they currently under that could explain their behaviour?

- Make a judgement as to the motives behind their behaviour. Are they frustrated with you because they feel that:

  - You are not driving as hard as they are towards a particular goal?

  - You are giving them too much or too little detail?

  - You won't make a decision without all the facts?

  - You leap to conclusions before you have all the facts?

- Are they themselves being bullied and mirroring this behaviour because it makes them feel better or more in control?

- Are they suffering from stress, or lacking in self-confidence or self-esteem?

- Are they struggling in their role and out of their depth?

- Do they have personal issues?

Once you have a handle on what is driving their behaviour, you will need to consider your strategy for dealing with the situation. Use the list from 'Dealing with the foxes of the world', Hints and Tips, Chapter 22 to help you devise your tactics.

Malice intended – these are the real bullies. They are capable of destroying their victims' self-esteem and making their lives a misery. First, I will offer some general advice and then move on to consider more specifically how to deal with each of the different types of bully.

Keep a factual log of every instance that you feel bullied. Keep copies of any documents that refer to you or your work in a negative light. Many incidents may appear trivial in isolation so it is important to establish a pattern over a period of time.

You will need this factual evidence when you confront your boss, ask for help or indeed if you make a formal complaint. In addition, writing things down often helps put the situation into perspective and can often make you feel better – more in control and more positive.

Get some help; talk to a trusted colleague or other manager, consult your HR department, your union representative or your safety representative. They may accompany you when you speak to the bully or see them on your behalf. They can also put you in touch with support groups and help you with a formal complaint if it goes that far. If the bullying is affecting your health, visit your GP. Remember this behaviour is not something you should or need to endure.

Keep positive, stay calm and be strong. Remember that criticism and personal remarks are not connected to your abilities. They reflect the bully's own weaknesses and are meant to intimidate and control you.

Now consider which category of bully your boss falls into. How clever are they? How much self-control are they able to exercise? Refer to the model in the previous section and then, according to their classification, consider the following, more targeted advice.

Dealing with the brutes – time alone will often expose this type of bully and show them up for what they are. Your best approach is to marginalise them, to cultivate relationships around them, and wait for the day when they reveal their true colours for all to see.

Dealing with the bouncers – speak to them, tell them that their behaviour is unacceptable and ask them to stop. This type of bully will not like to be confronted, particularly by someone who also has the ability to remain calm and civilised. Stick to the facts, but explain the impact of their behaviour and how it makes you feel. Help them to succeed, to develop their skills and to shine at something. Offer them the limelight.

Dealing with the runaway trains – praise their intellect, build on their suggestions and generally make them feel good about themselves. This will hopefully reduce their volatility. Make them feel comfortable with you by helping them to understand you. Be truthful, but also firm. Never be sloppy or slapdash.

Dealing with the schemers – with this type of bully the majority of the bullying behaviour goes on behind closed doors. Find out if they are doing the same thing to others; you may well find that you are not alone. Even if you are alone, the more people that know what your boss is doing to you, the more difficult it is for them to flourish. Do your homework on them – as they say, 'get to know your enemy'. When you understand their 'hot buttons' you may try, as a short-term measure, to make yourself useful, help them out, make them look good and massage their ego. In the meantime gather evidence, cultivate your network and engage the support of your allies and advocates. In the longer term, the only way of dealing with this type of bully is likely to be by making a formal complaint. However, before you do, make sure you have all your 'ducks in a row'.

And, finally, keep telling yourself 'I'm OK' – remember, the problem is with the bully, not you!

PART 5
TOOLS THAT WILL HELP

24 HOW TO MANAGE YOUR TIME TO MAXIMUM EFFECT

WHY IS THIS IMPORTANT?

Our time is a precious and a limited commodity. You buy other people's time to do things you do not want to do or cannot do and your time is bought by whomever you work for. Most people do not analyse where their time goes – a similar attitude to money is called reckless spending. Here are some thought-provoking adages on the subject of time:

- How we spend our days is, of course, how we spend our lives.
- The good people are already busy.
- Work always expands to fill the time available.

Most junior and middle managers never seem to have enough time to do all the things they want to do or think they ought to do. The middle managers I work with typically say they spend 20 to 30 per cent of their time dealing with their emails. Much of the rest of their time is spent in react mode responding to telephone calls, attending meetings, dealing with people that turn up on their doorstep, and so on – the list is endless.

As a manager, the most important motto of all for you to ponder is:

> If you can't manage yourself, you can't manage anyone else.

DELVING A LITTLE DEEPER INTO THE SUBJECT

Your aim is to be effective in what you do and efficient in the way you do it. However, it is very easy to confuse efficiency for effectiveness:

- Efficiency is time related; it is about doing things the right way.
- Effectiveness is goal related; it is about doing the right things.

Effectiveness is about doing those things that are important, the tasks, activities and decision-making that will help you to achieve your purpose and help build the organisation you work for, i.e. it is about doing the job you are employed to do and what you get paid for doing.

It is relatively straightforward to plan your time based on the urgency of a task; however, it is easy to forget to take into account the importance of a task. Generally speaking, important tasks are the ones that are likely to contribute towards your effectiveness.

Importance and urgency are two mutually independent measures; just because a task is urgent, it does not necessarily follow that it is important or vice versa. Based on these two measures, tasks therefore fall into one of four categories, as shown in the matrix in Figure 24.1 adapted from Covey's *The 7 Habits of Highly Effective People*.

Figure 24.1 Priority matrix

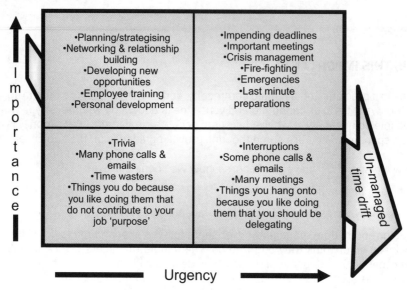

If you do not actively manage your time, it will tend to get swallowed up by activities that fall into the bottom-right quadrant; this is nearly always at the expense of activities in the top-left quadrant. The consequences of insufficient time in the top-left quadrant are re-work, fire-fighting and crisis management, which in turn leave even less time for planning and strategizing. A vicious circle sets in and we cease to become effective.

HINTS AND TIPS

In order to turn this vicious circle into a virtuous one, you need to ensure that you spend sufficient time in the top-right quadrant and minimise the time you spend in the other three. Go through your calendar for the last three months and see where you spent your time. Is the balance right? Are you spending sufficient time on strategic activities as opposed to tactical issues? Now read and act on the following pointers, repeat the calendar exercise in another three months' time and assess your progress.

Banish time thieves – these include junk emails or emails that people have copied you into just because they can, irrelevant meetings, meetings for meetings' sake or people that stop by just for a chat because they are bored.

- Turn off all email and mobile phone alerts. Set email filters to draw your attention to what is important and eliminate the spam. As far as possible, schedule certain times of the day to check and deal with your email rather than reacting to each and every alert.
- Do not have social network sites open on your desktop.
- Be selective about the meetings you attend; if you do not have a valuable contribution to make, decline the invitation.
- If you schedule a meeting, restrict it to 30 minutes with no more than seven participants.
- If someone drops by for a chat, tell them you only have a minute – if they need more, schedule them in at lunchtime or at the end of the day. Use non-verbal cues to indicate that their time is up – stand up or put your jacket on.

Concentrate – get to know your own body clock. If you are most productive in the morning, do those tasks that require more brainpower then; leave the phone calls that do not require a lot of thought until the afternoon when your energy levels are dwindling.

- Take mini beaks – a simple five-minute walk to the coffee machine can do wonders to recharge your batteries.
- Remember to eat – you need fuel to maintain your energy levels and the right type of fuel. Avoid heavy meals that take energy to digest and sugary snacks that cause your blood-sugar levels to yo-yo; instead, go for complex carbohydrates and small amounts of protein that provide you with a slow and sustained release of energy.
- Do one thing at a time – you can only concentrate effectively on one thing; therefore, only have one task in front of you at any one time and remove any distracting 'clutter'.

Delegate – you delegate tasks to grow the people who report to you and to create space in your diary for other activities. Effective delegation is not easy. The principal challenges are:

- The initial overhead when you delegate a task for the first time – it is probably true that, in the short term, you could do the task quicker and better yourself, but the consequences are that your people never learn to do new things and that you run out of time while they run out of work.
- Letting go of jobs that you like doing – this is called growing up.
- Learning to trust and overcoming the fear of losing control.
- Taking back jobs when a team member asks for help – you will discover that staff are very good at upward delegation, so make sure the ball stays in their court. Always remember that you can delegate responsibility and authority, but you cannot delegate accountability!

Turn to Chapter 2 for advice on effective delegation and Chapter 18 for advice on how to let go of jobs you like doing, but should no longer be undertaking.

Use the 80:20 rule – some things do need to be perfect, but more often than not 80 per cent is good enough. Many people, and in particular IT professionals, have a tendency to over-engineer and strive for perfection in all that they do. Ask yourself 'Is it fit for purpose? Will it do the job?' If the answer to these questions is yes then stop. Always have the Pareto Principle in the back of your mind, that 20 per cent of the effort will give you 80 per cent of the benefit.

Eliminate wasted time:

- Plan your time, schedule those important but non-urgent tasks and allow time to deal with all the day-to-day stuff that lands on your desk.

- Handle items only once – as far as possible deal with each email and piece of paper then and there; you will only waste time having to reread it at a later date. If you cannot deal with it then and there, save future time by making quick notes in relation to the salient points and actions you need to take to jog your memory.

- Utilise dead time – use travelling time to catch up on reading material or to relax with a good fiction book and waiting time to catch up on your emails.

- Avoid procrastinating over those things that you do not feel like doing because they are difficult, unpleasant or uncomfortable. Do them first – you will be amazed at how much better you feel and how much more productive you will be without the weight of an unpleasant task hanging over you.

- If you have a task that you are really struggling to get motivated to tackle try the 30-minute rule, it will help you get started. Start the task, but limit yourself to 30 minutes and then see how you feel. At worst you will have broken the back of the task, at best you may have achieved so much that you are motivated to continue to its completion.

- Be decisive – most of us waste plenty of time dithering over fairly trivial decisions; any decision is often better than no decision. If a course of action is taking you in the right direction then carry on; if it is not, remember you can always change course. Apply the 80:20 rule to information gathering; gather enough rather than striving for all that is available.

Get organised:

- Be realistic about what you can achieve in any one day. Ensure you leave time to get yourself organised, delegate effectively, deal with the day-to-day stuff, eat and have a little 'me' time in order to switch off and relax. Estimate the time needed for a task, not just the starting time. Remember that things often take longer than you think, so allow for this in your planning.

- Try to anticipate possible problems or difficulties in advance and also allow for these in your planning.

- Use a daily 'to do' list, do not include too many items and leave space for the unexpected. Maintain a second 'to do' list for longer-term tasks.

- Operate a one-place system – write everything down in one place, be it a tablet or notebook. If you need to refer back to who said what in a meeting or find a phone number, it will be there. It gets rid of the clutter and you will stop losing information. Personally, I prefer an old-fashioned notebook, it is in date order and easy to flick through. It also has the added bonus of opposing the IT stereotype.

- Chunk tasks – group similar tasks together and do them as a batch.
- Chop a big task down into smaller, more manageable pieces.
- Do not get side-tracked or distracted – if you think of something else you need to do while in the middle of another task, make a note so that you will not forget it, but complete the task you are currently working on first.
- Do not leave things to the last minute.
- Develop a filing system that works for you and use it. You will need to allocate a little time each day to keep it under control.
- Make appointments with yourself in your diary, this is the personal time you need to get organised and to operate in the top-left quadrant of the priority matrix. It will encourage you to spend the time how you intended and also avoid other people filling the spaces in your diary for you.
- Finally, do not let other people's lack of planning throw you off course. As one fiery secretary I know would say: 'Your lack of planning doesn't make it my emergency!'

Learn how to say 'no' – *the* vital thing to bear in mind is that you cannot possibly say 'yes' to everybody all of the time. It is far better to be honest and learn to say 'no' rather than 'maybe', 'if I can fit it in', 'possibly' or suchlike. Do not give people false hope; saying 'no' is better than saying 'yes' and then not being able to deliver. Be firm, be fair, be honest, be consistent and be polite. If it is your boss who is demanding your time, set out what you have to do and ask them to suggest a priority order, make sure they understand the potential consequences of any compromise they are asking you to make – write it down.

Handling your email – learn to use email appropriately.

- When messages are simple and straightforward, nothing can beat email; however, complex or ambiguous issues are always best dealt with face to face or at least over Skype or the telephone. This will save time and also reduce the risk of your message being misconstrued. Email can then be used to confirm the outcome of your discussions.
- Use the copy facility wisely and frugally and teach others, in particular your team members, to do the same.
- Make the subject line meaningful and flag emails for action in the subject line. Set an example and teach others to do the same.
- If you do get copied in on things that you do not need to know about, either delete them without reading beyond the subject line or file them in a 'just in case' file. Do not feel obliged to read each and every email you receive.
- Develop the ability to skim-read.

REFERENCE

Covey, S. (1989) *The 7 habits of highly effective people*. New York: Simon & Schuster.

25 DEVELOPING YOUR EMOTIONAL INTELLIGENCE

WHY IS THIS IMPORTANT?

The term 'emotional intelligence' was popularised by Daniel Goleman in 1995. There are numerous different models and measures of emotional intelligence, but essentially they all boil down to the same thing: an ability to understand and deal with your emotions and those of people around you.

Emotional intelligence is often measured as an Emotional Intelligence Quotient, or EQ for short. EQ describes an ability, capacity or skill to perceive, assess and manage the emotions of one's self, of others and of groups.

Being clever and having a high IQ will open doors to your chosen profession. However, once you are in that profession, EQ emerges as a much stronger predictor of who will be most successful; it is how we handle ourselves in our relationships that determines how well we do once we are in a given job. As a technician, EQ is a very important skill to have; however, as a manager EQ is an absolutely essential skill.

DELVING A LITTLE DEEPER INTO THE SUBJECT

Like so many aspects of human behaviour, there is no 'right' or comprehensive definition of the term emotional intelligence. My preferred set of characteristics is as follows:

- **Self awareness** – understanding yourself, your style, your values, your strengths and weaknesses, how you behave and respond to various situations. Being aware of the image you portray and your reputation. What makes you happy and what gives you a sense of 'fulfilment'.

- **Managing your emotions** – the ability to get yourself out of a negative state and to ensure that your bad mood does not have a negative impact on others. It is about avoiding making hasty judgements in the heat of the moment and not cutting off your nose to spite your face. It is about allowing others access to how you feel so that they can understand where you are coming from.

- **Focus** – knowing where you are going in life and having the drive and determination to get there. Having the emotional strength to cope with the setbacks in life and the tenacity to stick with things that are important to you even in the face of adversity.

- **Empathy towards others** – considering the feelings of others, being able to put yourself in their shoes, to sense and understand their viewpoints. Since up to 80 per cent of our communication is non-verbal, the ability to read facial expressions and body language is an important aspect of understanding the emotions of others. Being sincere and genuinely caring about others is another crucial aspect, as is valuing and appreciating differences.

- **Social skill** – the previous four abilities are the foundations for this, the fifth; social skill is where the real payoff occurs. It is about being able to build mutually beneficial and harmonious relationships with almost anybody you come across, even the most difficult individuals. It is about finding a win–win solution, no matter how apparently intractable it may appear.

HINTS AND TIPS

Many people who rely heavily on their intellect in their work neglect to develop their emotional intelligence. That is the bad news. The good news, however, is that, unlike IQ, which is an innate characteristic, EQ can be learned and developed.

Developing self awareness

Psychometric instruments have a useful part to play in developing self awareness, but, like any tool, they can be open to misinterpretations. They are useful for making sense of human behaviour and how you are likely to react in certain situations, but the output should not be taken too literally, nor should it be used to pigeonhole people.

Asking for feedback and accepting it with good grace is another important way of developing self awareness – see Chapter 3 for more detailed advice on asking for and receiving feedback.

Finally, allowing time for self reflection and analysis – how you behaved and dealt with various situations and the impact you had – will also provide you with valuable insights.

Self awareness is about personal honesty and about being comfortable with who you are.

Managing your emotions

When things are going well it is easy to stay positive. The real test of a positive nature, however, comes in the face of adversity when things start to go wrong. The clue is in how quickly you bounce back. You may find you have a moment or two when it all gets on top of you; you lose control, your composure slips and you feel the onset of despair. But when the moment is over, your fighting spirit comes back, your sense of humour recovers and you start to see the funny side; you make the best of the situation and take the proverbial bull by the horns.

When things are going wrong, some people try to ignore the situation – 'sticking your head in the sand' and ignoring the problem is not going to help it go away. The longer problems remain unaddressed, usually the worse they become. Problems need to be embraced, not ignored. If handled properly, problems can be the catalyst that helps you to see differently and adopt new thinking patterns. They are a powerful learning opportunity.

The question 'Did things go wrong or just not as planned?' is always a good one to have at the back of your mind. When you double-book yourself, your flight gets cancelled or a supplier delivers the wrong product, these are simply examples of life itself. You cannot live a life in which everything goes according to plan. It is the ups and downs, the unexpected twists, the moments of serendipity that keep us on our toes and provide us with those special moments and instances of inspiration.

Just as enthusiasm is infectious, so negativism is contagious; a negative attitude will spread like wildfire and have a knock-on effect to all of those around you.

Here are a few things you can do to help you stay positive when events conspire against you:

- Do not be frightened or too proud to ask for help – it is very easy to get so close to a problem that you cannot see the 'wood for the trees'. In such cases, someone else may be able to take a different perspective, to see a way through that is not obvious to you; as they say, two heads are better than one.

- Talk things through – when you articulate your fears, worries or concerns out loud, often they do not sound so bad. When you get things off your chest, it can make it easier to move on.

- When things go wrong (or not as planned), put the situation in perspective by asking yourself the following questions:

  - Is the world going to stand still because of this?
  - Can I have another go?
  - Can it be mended?
  - Can I buy a new one?
  - How much will this matter in one, five, ten years' time?
  - What are the alternatives?
  - What lessons can I learn?
  - Will I be remembered for this in my dotage?

These questions will help you to see that about 90 per cent of the things that you get worked up about are really rather trivial and in the grand scheme of things are not worth ruining your day over. Everyone has bad-hair days – do not blow them out of proportion, get over it and move on; remember the saying, 'there is no point crying over spilt milk'.

- Take time out – forget about your problems for a day; just go out and do something fun. Go to a movie, go for a ride on your bike or have a game of golf, anything that is completely different, that you enjoy and that fully absorbs your attention. Re-address the problem another day when you are re-energised and in a better place.

- Re-evaluate, not just the situation, but also your outlook on the situation. Instead of complaining about the plan that is not working out, make a new plan. Instead of griping about a procedure that failed to deliver the required outcome, analyse the reason why and develop a new and better procedure. Take action to create the best possible outcome rather than stressing over outcomes that are unattainable. Life tends to be a self-fulfilling prophecy – positive thoughts produce positive outcomes just as negative thoughts produce negative outcomes; you are either the master or the victim of your attitudes.

- Focus on what you can control or influence rather than what you cannot. It is a pointless waste of energy and mental capacity fretting and worrying about things that you cannot change; focus on what you can achieve rather than what you cannot. Do not let what you cannot do interfere with what you can do.

- Look on the funny side – humour helps you cope in difficult times and lightens the mood. For example, a friend, who had recently been the victim of a robbery, on telling the story concluded with the quip, 'we finally got rid of that awful figurine that my aunt bought us'. See Chapter 29 for more on maintaining a sense of humour.

- Do not give up – just because something went wrong once or failed, it is no reason to give up or not to try again. Use failure as a learning opportunity – 'Well at least I know not to try that again.' Remember Thomas Edison's famous saying, 'I did not fail. I just succeeded in finding 100 ways not to make a light bulb.'

- If you are under stress or pressure read the advice in Chapter 19.

- If you feel persistently sad, unmotivated, anxious, hopeless or fearful, it may be time to seek professional help.

Do not just wait for things to go wrong before you take action. The following everyday advice will help you to remain positive and look on the brighter side of life:

- Plan your day – this will help to improve your focus and prevent that overwhelmed feeling, provided that you are neither too ambitious nor too rigid. Ensure there is a little slack to enjoy some moments of relaxation, and delight in the serendipity of those chance encounters. Do not expect everything in life to go as planned; if you do, you will be quickly disappointed. See Chapter 24 for advice on time management.

- Look after your physical well-being – exercising, eating well and getting enough sleep will all contribute to a positive attitude.

  - Exercise is good for both mind and body; those endorphins improve your mood and provide you with that feel-good factor.

  - Nutrition – as they say, 'an army marches on its stomach'; if you are not getting the right fuel in sufficient quantities, you will find it more difficult to find the energy to keep positive when things are going wrong. Indeed, the 'B' vitamins are particularly important for your mental well-being.

- Sleep – you need sufficient sleep, the right amount for you. If you have problems getting to sleep, try some relaxation techniques (see below) just before you go to bed.

- Relaxation – people need to unwind from their busy lives. Try listening to your favourite music, reading a novel, watching a 'soap', taking the dog for a walk, meditation or other relaxation techniques such as tai chi.

- Inject some 'me' time into your life – no matter who you are or what you do, everyone needs a little 'me' time each day to recharge those emotional batteries. This is one of the single most important things that you can do for yourself, so start today. See Chapter 20 on how to achieve a satisfying work/life balance.

Focus

In order to maintain your focus and effortlessly give of your best there needs to be alignment between what you find yourself doing and what truly motivates you. If you are happy in your work, time will pass very quickly; if you are miserable in your work, time will pass very slowly. So how do you ensure that you are happy in your role?

The research almost always focuses on three variables: ability, values and life interests. One recent study found life interests to be paramount. The researchers argued that while ability can make you feel competent and you can be contented with the rewards that you receive, only life interests will keep most people happy and fulfilled over the long term. They defined these life interests as long-held, emotionally driven passions; the things you truly love doing and, if injected into your working day, are likely to increase job satisfaction and improve your motivation. In their *Harvard Business Review* paper, Butler and Waldroop describe eight 'deeply embedded life interests', or DELIs for short. They suggest that one, two or three of these drive most people. They are as follows:

- Application of technology – people with this life interest are intrigued by the inner workings of things. They are the ones who want to know how it works because the technology excites them, as does the possibility that it could be tinkered with and improved.

- Quantitative analysis – people with this life interest gravitate towards numbers. They love running the numbers and see it as the best way to figure out business solutions.

- Theory development and conceptual thinking – people with this life interest enjoy thinking and talking about abstract ideas; the 'why' interests them far more than the 'how'. They like thinking about situations from the '30,000-foot' level.

- Creative production – people with this life interest are frequently seen as imaginative, out-of-the-box thinkers. They thrive on newness and may take little interest in things that are already established.

- Counselling and mentoring – these people are drawn towards teaching and guiding others towards better performance; they are drawn to work situations that allow them to help others grow and improve.

- Managing people and relationships – people with this life interest prefer to work with and through people to accomplish the goals of the business. They thrive in line-management positions.

- Enterprise control – people with this life interest are happiest when they have ultimate decision-making authority. They feel great when they are in charge of making things happen.

- Influence through language and ideas – for people with this life interest, effective communication is more than a skill; it is a passion. They feel most fulfilled when writing or speaking; enjoyment comes from storytelling, negotiating or persuading.

If you can understand your own DELI or DELIs, you will be better able to recognise the things that will inspire and motivate you. Consider the impact your recent promotion to a manager has had on the fulfilment of your DELIs. To what extent does your new role build on and play to the strengths of your DELIs? Consider how you could re-define or enhance your role to ensure you utilise your strengths to the full and are able to express your DELIs as far as possible.

Empathy towards others

Empathy is about understanding others' feelings and emotions, being respectful of their values and point of view, listening without judging or forcing your point of view upon them, appreciating and valuing difference and, most importantly, not assuming that everyone is the same as you.

The ability to sense the feelings and emotions of others is an inherent skill as much as a learned one. Most of human evolution took place without language. Over millions of years we learned how to read non-verbal signals because these were all that were available to us. So, down there in your unconscious lies a whole range of abilities to recognise and respond to non-verbal signals, to read emotions in facial expressions and to interpret feelings through body posture. All you have to do is re-learn.

One excellent way of re-learning these skills is through the arts. When you read a work of fiction, watch a film or perform in a play, you are inviting your empathetic skills to play along with you. As you associate with the hero or villain, as you share the plight of the protagonists or as you get into role, you are putting yourself in someone else's shoes. This is excellent practice in developing empathy and will help you on the road to becoming fluent in body language.

Fluency in body language entails understanding both the signals you give to others and how they may be interpreted. It is also about being able to read others' thoughts and emotions through their gestures, posture and facial expressions. See the next section for more on body language.

Another key skill is to stop telling and to start listening. For many people, when faced with someone telling them about a problem or concern, their automatic reaction is to offer a solution to resolve that problem or concern. In such circumstances this is not what is needed – when someone is under emotional distress they need TLC (tender loving care) rather than a solution. When you have made them feel better by empathising

137

with them and providing TLC, they will then, in all probability, be capable of resolving their own problem or concern. Empathy is person centred rather than task focused. Developing your coaching and mentoring skills will help you learn to focus on the person rather than automatically diving into problem solving mode, see Chapter 28 for more details.

Social skill

One of the keys to success in social skill is the ability to find a win–win in almost every situation. This calls on all four elements of emotional intelligence described above. You need to be aware of how you feel about the other person; you need to manage your own emotions to positive effect; you need to focus on a mutually beneficial goal and have the emotional strength to cope with any setbacks or disagreements; and you will need to get under the skin of the other person to see things through their eyes as clearly as you see the situation through your own. In order to find a win–win you will need to listen, ask questions, build upon the ideas and thoughts of others and effectively handle any differences of opinion. At the same time you will need to pay attention to their body language and your status and make an effort to connect on a social level.

Actively listen – when in conversation with others, many people do not really listen to what the other person is telling them, rather they are focusing on what they are going to say next or the next question they are going to ask. Demonstrate that you are really listening and following the thread of a conversation with comments and questions such as:

- I think the same trend may be emerging in HR, Finance, etc.
- That is really interesting. I wonder if that solution is transferable to XYZ?
- How did you first notice XYZ?
- I wonder if others are seeing the same patterns.

If your attention wanders, a useful technique to help you concentrate on what the other person is telling you is to make notes of the key points of the conversation.

Ask questions – to understand where others are coming from; why they think and believe what they do; to gain new insights and new knowledge; to explore new possibilities; and to challenge existing paradigms. Encourage your audience to talk and open up by asking gentle, probing questions such as:

- What would we need to put in place for XYZ to happen?
- How might our customers feel if we could do XYZ?
- What would the competition say if they thought we could do XYZ?
- What else might we be able to do if we crack this one?
- Just how good could it get if …?

Build upon the ideas and thoughts of others – avoid being judgemental. Even if you think something is off the wall or daft, it may well be that if the thought is developed further you may see something you had not thought of. Avoid the use of the word 'but'; this is a put-down word. Replace it with the building word 'and'. Try comments such as:

- That sounds great; and can you explain a little more about how you went about it?
- Wow; and how did you hit upon an idea like that?
- I really like this approach; and do you think it might work in my department?
- I think that is a really interesting idea; and how do you think we could avoid the issue of XYZ?
- I can see the benefit; and how would we resource that?
- How do we build on the lessons we learned last time we tried that?

Look for links and connections between thoughts and ideas. Try questions and comments along the lines of:

- I wonder if there is a connection between X and Y?
- Might X have an impact on our ability to Y?
- If we could launch X in our key market, how might this affect our existing product lines?
- If we commit resources to this idea, what would be the potential knock-on impact to project Y?

Handling difference – there are two prime factors involved when it to comes to handling difference, these are:

- Assertiveness – the degree to which you try to satisfy your own concerns.
- Cooperativeness – the degree to which you try to satisfy the other person's concerns.

Your aim should be to be both assertive and cooperative, to work together to achieve a win–win outcome for both parties. This is called collaboration. In order to achieve this you will need to:

- Bring differences to the forefront and understand each other's point of view.
- Put your cards on the table and learn from each other's insights.
- Engage in brainstorming techniques to find alternative solutions that meet both sets of needs or concerns.
- Be firm, but also fair.

Collaboration should not be confused with compromising. Compromising is about cutting a deal, 'horse trading' or bargaining. The aim is to reach a middle ground, I give a bit, you give a bit. The result is a middle-ground position whereby neither parties' needs or concerns are truly met.

Pay attention to body language – being able to engage constructively with people is a real and valuable skill, but it takes more than just good verbal dialogue. Your manner and body language are equally important.

- Be warm and friendly in your approach; smile and make good eye contact.

- Avoid negative facial expressions such as frowns or raised eyebrows.

- Give them time to think and respond and signal that you are listening with encouraging noises and gestures.

- Keep an open, neutral posture, not too forward and 'in your face', and not too laid-back or macho; do not fold your arms or cross your legs – this creates a barrier.

- Avoid putting your hands in your pockets – this will also prevent you adopting the annoying male habit of jingling the loose change in there.

- Equally, avoid other distracting signals, such as wandering eyes, personal grooming or constant sniffing, as they will all reduce the effectiveness of your message.

- Practise your handshake; this needs to be firm but not too firm. There is nothing worse than either a limp-fish or bone-crusher handshake.

Learn how to read the body language of others.

- What do their facial expressions tell you – are they happy, sad, angry or nervous, for example. Is their smile a genuine one? Look at their eyes. As a general rule, when people are genuinely smiling the corners of their eyes as well as their mouth lift and crinkle; when the smile is fake only the mouth moves.

- What does their body posture convey – arrogance, intimidation, boredom, frustration, defensiveness and so on? Feet tapping, for example, may indicate frustration or irritation; turning their body away from you, leaning back and folding their arms may indicate that they do not like what they are hearing.

- Are they being truthful – in childhood a hand covering the mouth gesture is commonly an indication that a child is not being truthful, in adulthood this may be refined to a nose touching gesture.

- Is their body language in sync with their verbal message? When people mean what they say their body language normally reinforces their verbal message; however, when people do not verbalise what they really mean or feel, their body language may be at odds with their verbal message, unless of course they are skilled in the art of manipulation to avoid arousing suspicion. Next time you ask someone if they are 'OK' and they say 'yes', watch their body language, does this say the same thing? If not, say: 'Are you really sure, do you want to talk about it?'

- Be aware of mirroring. If someone mimics your body language this is often a very genuine sign that they are trying to establish rapport with you. Try changing your body position and see if they change theirs similarly, if they do they are mirroring. Equally, if someone adopts a negative body posture mirror them and then change your position to adopt a more positive posture. The likelihood is that they will follow suit – this technique is called, match, pace and lead.

Be aware of cultural differences and norms, you may need to adjust your body language to suit. Cultural norms regarding body language (i.e. how far away you should stand from someone, how much eye contact you should make and what gestures are considered taboo) vary considerably and if you do not speak the same body language as the locals, you are liable to be misunderstood and could cause offence.

Body language is a vast subject and the forgoing has barely scratched the surface. To do it justice I would need to write an entire book on the subject. There are many good books already in existence, so please see Further Reading for more guidance.

Status

You want to come across as open, accessible, approachable and strong, i.e. calm, confident and at ease. You do not want to appear weak and apologetic; neither do you want to appear aloof and arrogant.

In terms of status you therefore want to hit the middle ground, you will achieve this through your:

- Physical status – this should be proud, confident, straight and relaxed.
- Vocal status – calm and measured thought, clarity of speech at an acceptable/appropriate volume, not too loud and not too quiet.
    - Vary the pitch and pace of your speech to give light and shade to your delivery and make it more interesting.
    - Use an appropriate tone; tone is about resonance and intention and communicates emotion – excitement, passion, anger, disappointment, enthusiasm, etc.
    - Eliminate the 'ums' and 'ers'; audible pauses are not attractive, real pauses are great. Believe it or not, it is very interesting to watch someone who is not speaking!
- Mental status – being in the right frame of mind. Overcome anxiety or fear. Look and act the part.
- Use humour to oil the wheels of your conversation, to break any tension and to keep your audience interested and engaged. See Chapter 29 for more on the importance of humour.

As a final thought, consider the difference between confidence and arrogance. Confidence is knowing what you can do well; arrogance is not knowing what you cannot do well. Emotionally intelligent people are confident, emotionally illiterate people are often arrogant.

Connect with people on a social level

Look for common interests, hobbies, support of the same football team, children of the same age, attending the same school, etc. If you have something in common with somebody else they are far more likely to warm towards you – to consider you as their 'in-group'. See Chapter 21 for details on evolutionary psychology – how and why we evaluate and classify others.

26 HOW TO ENGENDER TRUST AND LOYALTY FROM OTHERS

WHY IS THIS IMPORTANT?

Trust and loyalty are the foundations on which relationships are built; they are the key to becoming part of a colleague's inner circle. Trust and loyalty work hand in hand, with loyalty emerging from the roots of trust. Once established, loyalty is a two-way street – when you demonstrate loyalty towards others, it generally comes back to you in spades.

Equally, loyalty and ethical behaviour go hand in hand. People are far more likely to invest their loyalty in you if you have a sound, unwavering moral and ethical compass. If people believe in you and trust you they are likely to do things for you gladly and will-ingly because they will want to help or please you. Without trust and loyalty your job as a manager will always be an uphill struggle of coaxing, cajoling and coercing others.

Every manager needs to know who they can trust and who will remain loyal to them, and the real test comes in difficult times.

> Be nice to people on your way up because you'll meet them on your way down.
> Wilson Mizner

DELVING A LITTLE DEEPER INTO THE SUBJECT

People often make the mistake of thinking that people approach them or recommend them because they are the most competent or able to do a job. Wrong. In most cases they approach or recommend you because they trust you and feel a degree of loyalty towards you.

Trust and loyalty take time to build. Trust only comes when you really get to know some-one, when you share common values, demonstrate mutual respect and care enough about the other person to put yourself out to help them. This means that you will have to be prepared to expose the real you, to allow people to see beyond your exterior veneer. It also means that you will need to be there for others when they need you most, not just when it is convenient for you or suits your purpose (see Chapter 26 for more on building trust).

Imagine you witnessed your boss or a trusted colleague going out on a limb or doing something that every sane person thinks is ethical, but foolhardy. Rather than running away so that none of the resultant 'mud' sticks to you, this would be your opportunity to step forward and lend your support. This is how you demonstrate true loyalty and how you engender loyalty from others.

HINTS AND TIPS

The quickest and simplest way to build trust is always to do what you say you will do; to ensure words and deeds are always congruent.

> If you say you are going to do something for someone
> Do it
> Actions speak louder than words

Never give people false hopes. If you cannot guarantee, do not promise. Neither should you make empty promises, nor just agree because you believe it is the polite thing to do. If you do not really mean something, and do not genuinely intend to act upon your words, do not say it!

Being loyal is about being helpful and supportive and making a personal sacrifice to help someone; it is about looking out for them, protecting their back and being prepared to put your own reputation on the line for them.

In public you should always speak well of your team and your colleagues and, if need be, you defend their actions. In private it is your job and your duty to give them feedback to challenge the ethical and moral grounds of their actions and decisions and to help them reflect on the outcomes of their actions so that they can develop into better people.

Consider the story of two admirals:

In their book on corporate cultures, authors Deal and Kennedy tell the story of the power of mutual recognition. Two junior officers in the Dutch Navy made an agreement that, on every social occasion they found themselves at, each would sing the praises of the other. They appeared to have no ulterior motive for speaking well of the other and this had a significant effect, revealed only when they were both made admirals – the two youngest admirals ever appointed in the Dutch Navy.

Try to make your colleagues look good. Or, if you cannot do this, at least make sure that you do not say nor do anything that makes them look bad. Never put anyone down, try to score points or belittle them either in public or in private. It is not gracious and although people may smile at the time, they are making a mental note that you are not to be trusted.

Be generous, give a little of yourself to others – your time, your expertise, your knowledge, your help, your support – without expecting anything in return.

Be prepared to forgive and forget, offer people a face-saving route if they need to change their minds or behave differently.

Of the people that you work closely with, ask yourself what keeps them awake at nights and whether you have it in your power to make them rest easier.

REFERENCE

Deal, Terrence E. and Kennedy, Allan A. (1982) *Corporate cultures: The rites and rituals of corporate life*. Reading, MA: Addison-Wesley Publishing Company.

27 HOW TO MANAGE YOUR PERSONAL DEVELOPMENT

WHY IS THIS IMPORTANT?

It is important to understand that you own your own career; your employer just affords you the opportunity to follow that career on their premises. This being the case, if you sit around waiting for your employer to develop you and your career, you will, invariably, wait a long time. Even if you are lucky enough to work for one of those enlightened organisations that trumpet their commitment to career development and talent management – you have to get recognised as 'talent' before you can even start to ascend their greasy pole.

The next most important thing to recognise is that growth cannot happen without learning. Learning needs to be both discipline and industry-sector related, but perhaps most importantly you also need to develop your emotional intelligence. As discussed in Chapter 25 this is likely to be the key to your future success.

Learning is not an event; it is a lifelong journey. Do not associate learning with attending a course, but rather think about your learning as an ongoing cycle of action and reflective enquiry.

All life's experiences are learning opportunities, whether they are positive or negative experiences; the most powerful lessons often come from learning from your mistakes. IT has a reputation of being very bad at learning from its mistakes, repeating them time after time.

DELVING A LITTLE DEEPER INTO THE SUBJECT

As a new manager you need to learn how to manage. You may have been sent on some management training courses, you may have been allocated a mentor to help to show you the way, but in all likelihood you will have been thrown in at the deep end and just expected to get on with it. A sink or swim approach.

If you are one of the lucky ones, take advantage, but do not rely or depend upon any such gifts. At the end of the day it is your responsibility to develop yourself to become the best manager you can possibly be. As a manager you will need an additional skill-set to the one that has served you previously – this skill-set is detailed in Part 1 of this book.

You may have just reached the position to which you aspire or you may, in time, be looking for the next, and the next, step up. Whatever the case, focus initially on learning how to do your current job well, learn the art of management and, when you are ready, broaden your horizons to open up new possibilities and opportunities for both you and your team. Ensure you get the balance right between hard and soft skills. As a new manager your initial focus is likely to be on the softer skills.

HINTS AND TIPS

All life's experiences are an opportunity to learn and grow. Children are very good at learning: they ask questions, they touch and play with things, they learn by trial and error, they are not fearful of making mistakes and they are not challenged by newness.

As adults we tend to take a more cautious approach. You will, in all probability, have been taught to consider the risks, to value the tried and tested and to strive for perfection in all that you do. You have amassed a significant amount of knowledge and know-how, you are under pressure to deliver and you are pushed for time, therefore you get busy with the day-to-day pressures of life and you stop asking questions or standing back to consider the bigger picture.

In order to learn you will need to keep an open mind and adopt a learning mindset where you take the most from life's experiences and actively seek additional opportunities to learn.

- Learn from your mistakes – be self-critical, but do not dwell on your mistakes, take the lesson and move on. Chalk it up to experience 'at least I've learned not to do it that way'. Ask for feedback on your current performance and then reflect on what that feedback is telling you. See Chapter 3 for advice on asking for and receiving feedback.

- Ask questions – adults have a tendency to overestimate their knowledge; this prevents you asking questions to check and confirm understanding and to gain new insights and perspectives. Never assume, always check, ask open questions of enquiry rather than closed questions that limit the response. You will be pleasantly surprised at the new insights you will gain. Stand back and ask the big questions: 'What is the purpose of this?' and 'Why do we do it this way?' or even 'What would happen if we didn't do it at all?' Just because you have always done something in the past it does not necessarily follow that you should continue doing it in the future. Never be concerned about asking a 'silly' question – there will almost certainly be someone else in the room wanting to ask the same thing.

- Watch and learn from others – how does your boss manage you? Which aspects of their style or behaviour do you appreciate the most and which do you appreciate the least? You will find some aspects that you may wish to emulate; you may also learn what not to do. Who do you look up to and why? These are your role models within your organisation – watch and learn from them.

- Get a mentor – if this is something your company offers, take advantage, if it is not, ask for one either formally or informally. A mentor is someone with greater experience than you, someone who can show you the way if you get stuck and someone you can use as a sounding board. They should provide reassurance or affirmation and boost your confidence in your new role. Make sure the mentor is the right person, someone you look up to. Systems that 'allocate' a mentor are unlikely to generate successful relationships.

- Identify training courses that you would benefit from.

- Attend conferences – in particular those that attract people from different industries or professions.

- Read books, papers and journals. Do not restrict yourself to your own professional discipline; increase the breadth of your reading. Try reading some popular literature explaining developments in biotechnology, genetics or finance. Read eclectic journals such as *Harvard Business Review*, *Nature*, *The Economist*, *Fast Company*, *Sloan Management Review*, and so on.

- Broaden your experience and hence your horizons:

  - Find opportunities to spend time working in other departments and look to rotate your staff through various roles and departments.

  - Volunteer to serve on cross-functional initiatives, whole-organisation changes, etc.

  - Take an interest in what other departments are doing and try to understand the values that underpin their initiatives.

  - Understand the end-to-end nature of the processes that your department is engaged in. Where do the inputs come from, where do your outputs go and how are they used? Think along the time line as well as the process flow.

  - Get into the habit of having lunch or coffee with people from different disciplines or different departments from yours.

  - Take up a new hobby, one that is likely to expose you to different cultures and ways of thinking. Try your hand at amateur dramatics, for example.

  - Consider some form of higher education, but do it in a discipline that you have little or no experience of. Go and study the history of art or something else so different that it will give you a whole new perspective.

- If you have been assigned a mentor, at some point you may feel that you have outgrown them – this is the time to get a coach instead. It is important to understand that, when choosing a coach, you are not looking for someone who can tell you what to do. You are looking for someone who can listen to your experiences and then ask you really good questions; questions that make you think and motivate you to learn and do things differently.

The key to personal development is self reflection, learning and the courage to try something new. By all means take pride in doing something well, but always remain alert to the possibility that maybe you could have done it differently. Be aware of why you do what you are doing and learn to recognise when you need to start doing something differently. You probably have lots of technical qualifications; if you can, sign up for a management qualification that will give you more insights into the topics in this book and thereby demonstrate that you are keen to develop this side of yourself.

28 COACHING SKILLS

WHY IS THIS IMPORTANT?

Coaching is a very valuable managerial technique. It is beneficial for both developing and growing people and also for dealing with performance and motivational issues. Coaching is primarily aimed at those who have the 'skill' (see Figure 2.1, Skill versus will matrix). When you coach someone you are assuming they have the ability to work things out for themselves with a bit of encouragement and support. As a manager, your job is to provide this encouragement and support.

In my experience of working within the IT discipline and with IT people for the past 40 years, coaching is a very under-utilised skill. The majority of IT managers take a far more directive approach, this may well be appropriate with more junior staff, those who do not have the 'skill' (see Figure 2.1), but is highly de-motivational when applied to experienced people.

DELVING A LITTLE DEEPER INTO THE SUBJECT

Coaching requires a number of underpinning skills. These can easily be remembered by the acronym RACE (relationship building, active listening, constructive feedback, effective questioning):

- **Relationship building** – if you want to get someone to open up and to be prepared to work with you, you will need a trust-based relationship and to establish a good rapport.

- **Active listening** – when you listen properly to someone you will increase their ability to express themselves. When you actively listen to someone you need to put them centre stage and let go of your own thoughts and self-importance.

- **Constructive feedback** – feedback needs to be constructive, motivating and balanced. In the context of coaching you will always need to keep the thought in the back of your mind that the development of others is of prime importance.

- **Effective questioning** – this is the essence of coaching; by asking the right type of questions you tap into your coachees' thought processes and take them on a voyage of self-discovery and self-help.

Once you have developed the above skills, the GROW (goals, reality, options, wrap up) model will help you to structure a coaching intervention:

- **Goals** – the objective to be achieved.
- **Reality** – examining the issues or opportunity to be addressed.
- **Options** – identifying the available options.
- **Wrap up** – agreeing actions.

HINTS AND TIPS

Coaching is a vast subject, so again I can only hope to scratch the surface in this chapter. I am not trying to turn you into a professional coach, but, by applying the Pareto Principle introduced in Chapter 24 – that 20 per cent of the knowledge will give you 80 per cent of the benefit – learning the basics will reap significant rewards.

Your first step is to develop the skills that an effective coach needs. The following advice is structured around the RACE model.

Relationship building

Advice on building relationships, rapport and trust has been largely covered in previous chapters of this book. See Chapter 14 on relationship management, Chapter 8 on effective communication and building rapport and Chapter 26 for advice on how to build trust.

Remember, you cannot force someone to be coached so it must be elective and built upon a foundation of trust.

Active listening

This is easier said than done. It requires concentration, mindfulness, authenticity, openness, receptivity and intuition. When you really focus on someone else with the intention of fully listening to them, the sense of yourself will diminish and you will start to see the world through their eyes, this is empathy in action. See Chapter 25 on emotional intelligence for more advice on active listening and demonstrating empathy towards others. Remember, what stops you from listening in any situation is you; either you get distracted by your own thoughts or ideas, or you simply do not make the effort to focus on someone else. Therefore, resist any temptation to give your own examples of a similar situation, as this turns the attention away from them and back to you.

Constructive feedback

Again, this topic has already been covered in significant detail in Chapter 3; but always remember, you can criticise someone's behaviour but you should never criticise them as a person.

Effective questioning

Effective questions are worded so that the person answering only needs to work on forming their response rather than trying to understand the question. Effective questions also have a clear sense of purpose; for example, to gather more information, see something from another perspective or create a sense of the future. You will find examples of six different types of coaching questions below.

The first pair of questions are best used to gather more information or to explain, describe and clarify events:

- **Analytical questions** – these seek to explore cause and effect. They may take the form:

  - What, specifically, is it that you are unhappy with about ...?
  - What sequence of events preceded ...?
  - What might happen if we integrate ... with ...?

- **Probing questions** – these invite more detail and can be used to open up thinking or clarify a situation. They may take the form:

  - Can you tell me more about ...?
  - Who else may be able to throw light on this one?
  - What was the first thing you noticed when ...?

The next pair of questions are used to explore context and the social and emotional structures within which we operate:

- **Reflective questions** – these questions are introspective and individual. They challenge people to think about why they hold the views they do and to examine their motivations. They may take the form:

  - Why do you believe that ...?
  - What are your key concerns about ...?
  - What would need to change for you to feel comfortable about ...?

- **Affective questions** – are used to extract information about how people feel on a topic – they bring out the emotional aspects of a situation. They may take the form:

  - Why was there such resistance to our changes to the ...?
  - How is the change in ... impacting morale?
  - What would it feel like to work in an organisation that ...?

The final pair of questions are used to challenge conventional thinking and generate new ideas. If phrased well they can act as a powerful catalyst to change:

- **Explorative questions** – open up new avenues of enquiry and look for potential synergy. They may take the form:

  - What new things would you be able to achieve if ...?
  - Who else could benefit from ...?
  - What else could you do that would make this even more ...?

- **Fresh questions** – challenge 'eternal truths' and basic thinking – they are used for assumption busting. They can lead to breakthrough ideas and innovation. They may take the form:

  - Why can't you just ...?
  - From our customers' point of view what is the 'job to be done'?
  - If you could start with a blank sheet of paper how would you ...?

You will note that all the questions above are open in their intent and not leading or restricted by an anticipated answer. Using questions like this is not an easy skill and needs practice. But remember that questions trigger action so you need to ask the right questions to trigger the right actions. Your role as coach is to help your coachee shape their thoughts, reflections and ideas into an appropriate way forward that helps them grow.

If your coachee gets stuck for ideas help them by:

- Giving them time to reflect – a short period of silence may help.
- Asking a more general question – 'What are your options?' or 'What thoughts are you having now?'
- If they are looking confused or overloaded, a gentle summary by you will give them a short rest. Alternatively, you could take a break and go for a coffee.
- If not enough information has arisen you could ask: 'Last week, I heard you say ..., can you say a little more about that?'
- If they are focusing on the barriers or constraints of a situation, encourage them to think more positively by asking them: 'In an ideal world ...?' or 'What would you do if you were in the CEO's shoes?'

Now you have the necessary skills, the next step is to structure your coaching discussions. There are many models to help you with this, the most common is probably the GROW model.

Goal – this is your objective, how you wish to develop your coachee, what performance issue you want to address or how you want them to behave differently.

Reality – this is where you need to engage in dialogue about the objective. This is the most important stage of the process and where you should focus the vast majority of your time. Your questioning skills will come to the fore during this stage. You may well ask some probing questions to challenge your coachee's thinking and behaviour, you may ask some reflective questions to get them thinking about why they did what they did or some explorative questions to find out where they see themselves in three years time, for example. You should also ask questions to encourage your coachee to examine honestly the motives that underpinned their actions or desires.

If the objective is related to a performance issue, you may ask your coachee to think through the impact of their actions on others with an affective question. Try to keep the conversation success based and future focused; do not dwell on past performance.

Options – once the issues or opportunities have been identified, you, as the coach, will continue to ask questions to identify the potential options. You may offer suggestions at this point, but do it in a way that encourages your coachee to probe your thinking and build on your ideas. Make sure that you agree on a mutual course of action before you move on.

Wrap up – summarise what you have understood and what you have agreed. Talk frankly about what could get in the way of doing these things and ask your coachee what you can do to help. Agree what specific actions your coachee will take away from the meeting, who will make the next move and what it looks like.

29 THE IMPORTANCE OF MAINTAINING A SENSE OF HUMOUR

WHY IS THIS IMPORTANT?

The IT community is not generally noted for its sense of humour. When IT professionals do display a sense of humour it is often described in a somewhat negative sense; as 'dry' or 'cutting'. However, humour has many positive benefits in the workplace; many, and that includes myself, would say that it is an absolutely essential ingredient. It can be used to:

- bond people – something shared;
- diffuse tension and lighten the mood;
- oil the wheels of conversation;
- increase the impact of your words;
- aid creativity and understanding;
- increase your allure, i.e. it makes people want to associate with you – to share your company!

In addition, laughing delivers positive physiological benefits; it reduced the stress hormone, cortisol, and increases the infection-fighting lymphocytes in the blood stream. It reduces the heart rate and blood pressure and relaxes the muscles in the chest and shoulders. So there is a lot of truth in the saying 'laughter is the best medicine'.

DELVING A LITTLE DEEPER INTO THE SUBJECT

Like many emotions, those associated with laughter are contagious. Good humour can spread throughout a group – so long as people are prepared to be receptive. When people say 'this is too serious a matter to laugh about it', maybe the better response would be 'this is too serious a matter *not* to call upon laughter to help us out'.

Genuine humour depends upon a willingness to let go. It starts with the ability to laugh at oneself, laughing at the misfortunes of others is a grim surrogate for genuine humour. As human beings, we are all fallible. Some people deal with their fallibility by being defensive, pretending that they have no significant faults. Others, who have learned to lighten up, use their fallibility to their advantage.

No one is perfect. Those who strive for the impossible – personal perfection – are missing the point. Your aim should be to become the best possible version of you, to celebrate your uniqueness, your quirks and peculiarities, and to share with others the humour of your imperfections rather than try, vainly, to cover them up.

Success as a manager is about building trust and alliances. It is about being liked and respected more than being right or perfect. What makes us likeable is being human, fallible yet strong enough to see ourselves as others see us. It is also about being authentic, happy about who you are and comfortable in your own skin. The personal honesty, which I explored in greater depth in Chapter 25, is most obvious in those who can laugh at themselves. Having a sense of humour is attractive to others; it will make you more popular and more successful. In my own research, 95 per cent of chief executives said that they were more likely to recruit or promote someone with a good sense of humour than someone without one.

HINTS AND TIPS

You do not have to be good at telling jokes to be humorous. Indeed, jokes can often go wrong – particularly if they are directed at the misfortunes of others – and they do not translate well across cultural boundaries.

Learn to appreciate witty wordplay, puns and irony. Comedy often comes from linguistic confusions or playfulness – when there is a gap between words and meaning or expectation. Indeed, Freudian slips are linguistic errors that are believed to expose what you are really thinking rather than what you 'meant' to say.

Children are, unintentionally, very good at this type of humour. They naturally express humour from kindergarten age. So the ability lies within you – you just need to learn to nurture it and to trust your inner child.

If someone makes a linguistic slip, demonstrate your appreciation of the humour in it rather than correcting their mistake. Embrace the richness and whimsy of the English language. Consider, for example, the glorious and fanciful words that have been used for centuries to describe groups of birds:

- A wisdom of owls.
- A murder of crows.
- A mischief of magpies.
- A quarrel of sparrows.
- A conspiracy of ravens.
- A committee of terns.
- A banditry of titmice.
- A scold of jays.
- A charm of goldfinches.
- A deceit of lapwings.

Do not take yourself too seriously – be prepared to share those embarrassing moments in your life. Develop a self-deprecating sense of humour – others will find this endearing and a refreshing relief from those people who come across as touchy, prissy, precious or easily offended.

Learn from others; whether they are professional comedians, your parents, your kids or your boss, learning from the funny people in your life is a key step to being funny yourself. Watch comedy programmes on TV, attend an improvisation show, listen to comedy podcasts, read the works of authors such as P. G. Wodehouse and Douglas Adams and take out a subscription to magazines such as *Private Eye* or *The New Yorker*. You will be amazed as to what will rub off.

Consider humour as an intellectual challenge. In a way, being funny is simply showing that you are intelligent enough to find the humorous nuances that others miss.

Never forget that a little humour will give you the strength to carry on, and massively enhance your interpersonal skills. Our time on this planet is limited and finite, so let go, learn to experience the lighter side of life, to bring happiness to the people you interact with and live life to the full!

30   FINAL WORDS

I feel privileged to have lived in unique times. As someone who was born in 1956 I have witnessed the introduction of computers into our lives from the very beginning. At school I used logarithmic tables, during my first year at university I used a slide rule, by my second year hand held calculators had just become affordable.

I first learned to code in Fortran IV and submitted a stack of punch cards for batch programming each evening. The following morning, after my program had crashed, I would receive a 'core dump' to help me diagnose the errors in it. Over time the core dump would get smaller (providing of course my fellow students had not shuffled my punch cards while I was not looking) and eventually my program would work.

I witnessed the first dumb terminals with a VDU and the first PCs. I personally pioneered the introduction of computers onto the shop floor for the first time at Vickers Shipbuilding and Engineering. For 18 months I ran BT's Information Centre in the North East District putting PCs into the business for the first time and introducing their uses to 'End User Computing'. I observed the transition from memos to internal mainframe based email and subsequently to email as we know it today. I wrestled with such issues as data security and disaster recovery and convincing the business that we needed to spend money on such precautions. I was a part of the fear and in some cases panic leading up to the millennium and the huge anti-climax that followed.

The pace of change has been rapid and the need for people to adapt to new ways of working had never been so dramatic. In the shipyard I was teaching my predecessors how to use a computer, a generation who had grown up without technology – this was a situation unique to those days. The only way this would work is to take the people with you, to listen to their fears, to respect their status and be sensitive in your approach. I was fortunate to find that this came naturally to me (I am an 'idealistic' type) and as a consequence my projects were a success and my reward was a series of successive promotions within a rapidly growing IT function.

During my time in IT I have had many managers, both good and bad; both kinds have been a source of learning and inspiration. In my experience within IT the number of bad managers far exceeded the good. I hope that, by sharing my knowledge, experiences and the wisdom I have gained over the years, I can help you to become a good manager and in time a great leader. In order to become a great leader you will need to develop and acquire the:

- knowledge and know-how to show people the way;
- curiosity to ask searching questions, to learn constantly and to be open to new experiences;
- vision to know where you are going;
- courage to challenge authority and accepted wisdom;
- passion to inspire and motivate others;
- empathy to exercise compassion, consideration and to engender trust and loyalty.

This is my definition of great leadership and the good news is that you can learn all of this; the only prerequisite, in my opinion, is the passionate desire to become a great leader.

So, go forth and lead and may I wish you all the very best in your future endeavours.

APPENDIX:
YOUR FIRST 90 DAYS AS A NEW MANAGER

PREPARATION

You may be a new hire or you may have been promoted from within. If you are the former you should start even before you take up your new position. Study the organisation's website, read all the recent news that you can find about the organisation, its competitors and the challenges facing their industry sector. Study the history of the organisation and the biographies and LinkedIn profiles of the key executives. If you have been promoted from within, hopefully you will have much of this knowledge already, make sure you fill in any gaps. This will help you hit the ground running. You need to gain the knowledge and understanding to move up the political model depicted in Figure 22.1, Chapter 22.

Decide on your key objectives for your first 90 days. These should include:

- Watching, listening, learning and, in the process, gaining an understanding of:

    - your team members, your manager, your customers, your suppliers and other key stakeholders or decision makers within your organisation;

    - what is keeping these people awake at night;

    - the culture of the organisation and the various sub-cultures within;

    - the power structure within your organisation – both formal and informal;

    - the strategic objectives of your organisation and the challenges ahead;

    - hot topics, pressing issues and key priorities;

    - people's views and opinions of the IT function, i.e. IT's reputation;

    - the key challenges facing IT.

- Build relationships with everyone you meet and get key people onside (see Chapter 14 for advice on relationship building).
- Get some quick wins under your belt.
- Develop a strategy and plan for going forward after your 90-day 'honeymoon' period.

MAKING A START

Your first priority is to talk to your team and your boss. On day one schedule a meeting with your boss and each member of your team. Talk to each of your team members separately and allow enough time to get them to relax and open up. I would recommend that you schedule two and a half hours for each discussion – most sessions will not last this long, but you do not want to cut your people off if they are in mid flow.

Ask your team members to tell you about:

- their role;
- what aspects they enjoy most;
- what aspects they enjoy least;
- what they would change if they could;
- how IT functions on a day-by-day basis and the key interfaces with other departments/external providers;
- what works well and what does not work so well;
- what you should be most concerned about;
- your key stakeholders – who are your allies and who are the difficult customers;
- how they like to be managed;
- anything else that you should know about that you have not already asked.

Ask your boss to tell you about:

- how IT functions on a day-by-day basis and the key interfaces with other departments/external providers;
- what works well and what does not work so well;
- what keeps them awake at night;
- what you should be most concerned about and what your key priorities should be;
- what they expect from you and how they will measure your success;
- their management style and how they like to be communicated with – at this point take the opportunity to tell them how you like to be managed and your preferred communication style;
- your key stakeholders – who are your allies and who are the difficult customers;
- their impression of each member of your team;
- who else they think you should talk to;
- any recent surveys or performance measures relevant to it;
- anything else that you should know about that you have not already asked.

THE ART OF IT MANAGEMENT

Depending upon their answer to the previous questions, assess their enthusiasm for undertaking an 'IT health check' (see the final section to this chapter, Taking Stock). This would provide you with extremely valuable information on a variety of performance measures, a benchmark to measure your future successes against, data to compare yourself with the average across all industry sectors and also significant kudos for taking the initiative – all in one package.

Your second priority is to talk to your customers. You should ask them:

- how well IT serves them – what works well, what the problem areas are, what more IT could do;
- about their plans, priorities and challenges for the future;
- their number one priority;
- what they expect from their IT department;
- the relationship between IT and the other business functions;
- who else they think you should talk to;
- anything else that you should know about that you have not already asked.

You should also try to engineer informal interactions, over a coffee maybe, with:

- your CIO or head of IT;
- your CEO (if you work for a small organisation);
- your peer group;
- your key suppliers.

These discussions will serve two very important purposes – to gather information while building relationships in the process. Observe, ask questions and listen to everyone you meet; be a sponge. Make sure you say 'hi' to everyone around the office and that you put on a nice smile, offer a firm handshake and be positive. Avoid over-familiarity or snap judgements; keep your opinions to yourself until you are sure of your ground. Make yourself available and ingrain yourself in the culture of your organisation; if a peer or key stakeholder asks you to go out for a coffee or a drink after work, go without hesitation. Try to map the informal connections within the organisation – who talks to who, who listens to who, who goes to who for help, who has lunch with who or goes for drinks after work with who?

Read the business strategy and the IT strategy; if either does not exist go and talk to the key players and get them to articulate their thoughts verbally.

PUTTING IT ALL TOGETHER

Your next step is to build a picture of the current state of affairs. Make use of management tools to help structure your thoughts. You may consider using the SWOT (strengths, weaknesses, opportunities, threats) analysis; the project portfolio shown in Figure 15.1, Chapter 15, and the systems analysis shown in Figure A.1.

Figure A.1 Systems analysis

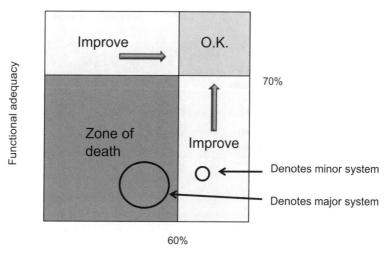

Technical adequacy

THE FINALE

Your final step is to demonstrate initiative and take action – remember, actions speak louder than words.

Look for some quick wins – this will help get people onside. Do not be afraid to do some personal, but work orientated, 'favours' for key influencers or adversaries of IT. Avoid major changes within your first 90 days and be cautious with any criticisms as to the way things are. Things might not have been perfect, but they worked before your arrival in your new role and you never know what may be construed as a personal criticism; demonstrate humility and show some professional courtesy.

At the 90-day point be ready with your analysis of the current situation and your plans for the future. Identify a 'reach' project that will add significant value to the business and that will make your boss look good. This will help to cement your relationship with your new boss and start to build your reputation.

If you have undertaken the IT health check (see the following section, Taking Stock) this is the time to use it – use it to evaluate current strengths and weaknesses and as a platform for action. Use the matrix in Figure A.2 to prioritise your initiatives.

Figure A.2 Prioritising opportunities

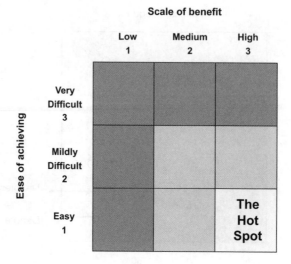

ADDITIONAL HINTS AND TIPS

Do not forget, as a new manager, that you have the opportunity to bring a fresh perspective and a unique opportunity to air your views – being new to a role gives you a lot of leeway.

Role model the behaviour you expect from others, everyone will be watching your technical etiquette. Emails should stay professional and your personal phone should be on silent or switched off. Be reliable; arrive on time, respect deadlines and deliver on promises. Demonstrate your commitment to the job.

You will invariably have lots of little questions. Do not bother your boss with the trivia, find yourself a mentor who will help you settle into your new role.

TAKING STOCK – THE IT HEALTH CHECK

If appropriate undertake an IT 'health check'. I developed this tool while lecturing at Cranfield School of Management. Over the years it has helped more than 60 organisations, both large and small and across all industry sectors. The tool is designed to pinpoint areas of strength and weakness. It also examines performance of an IT function at three different levels:

- **Level 1** – IT's ability to deliver the basics, i.e. robust and reliable systems in support of business needs. **Service delivery** is your licence to exist as an IT function; get this wrong and you are 'ripe' for outsourcing.

- **Level 2** – IT's ability to add value to the business, and to act and be seen as a **change agent**. At this level you are the engine of innovation; you will achieve this by asking better questions rather than searching for better answers to existing questions. This is your 'licence to influence'.

- **Level 3** – IT's ability to transform business thinking, and to act and be seen as a **business partner**. At the very top of the pyramid you will be helping to shape the future direction of your organisation and will have achieved your 'licence to decide'.

An example of the output is shown in Figure A.3.

As you can see from Figure A.1, you can easily pinpoint the areas of strength and the areas of concern, and where IT and the rest of the business are in alignment of their views and where they are not. I would normally present this output in colour using a traffic light coding system, i.e. sinking would be indicated by red (as opposed to dark grey), drifting would be indicated by amber (as opposed to pale grey) and cruising would be indicated by green (as opposed to white).

In the next section, you will find a questionnaire, a scoring key and benchmarking data drawn from over 1,500 respondents. Feel free to use and adapt these to your needs. If you would like soft copies please email the author at robina@chatham.uk.com.

IT HEALTH CHECK QUESTIONNAIRE

Listed in Figure A.4 are some statements relating to your view of *your* IT function. Please use the scale to respond to each statement. Place a number from 1 to 7 in the space just before each of the items.

Figure A.3 Example output from an IT health check

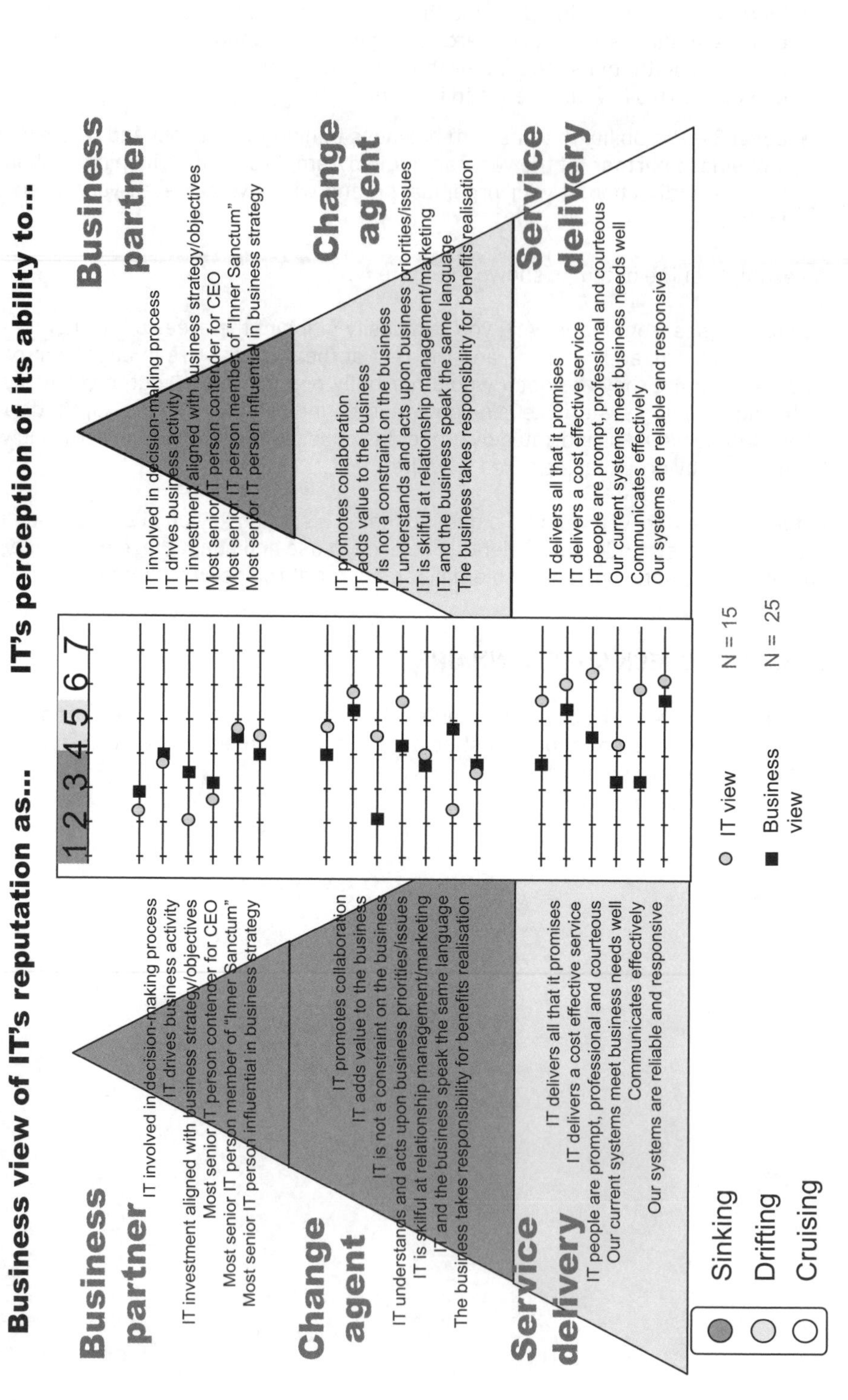

Figure A.4 IT health check questionnaire

Strongly disagree 1 2 3 4 5 6 7 Strongly agree

___1 The business takes full responsibility for the realisation of business benefits.

___2 The most senior IT person is influential in the formulation of business strategy.

___3 IT is skilful in managing customer relationships and markets itself well.

___4 IT communicates effectively with its customers.

___5 Our existing information systems meet the day-to-day needs of the business well.

___6 The most senior IT person is a respected member of the 'inner sanctum'.

___7 IT actively promotes an environment of collaboration with the business community.

___8 IT investment is aligned with business strategy and objectives.

___9 IT is actively involved in the business decision-making process.

___10 IT delivers all that it promises.

___11 IT is a fundamental driver of our future business activity.

___12 All members of the IT function provide a prompt, professional and courteous service to their customers.

___13 The IT function understands and acts upon business priorities and issues.

___14 Our systems are reliable and responsive.

___15 IT delivers a cost effective service.

___16 IT and the business speak the same language.

___17 IT adds value to the business.

___18 IT is not a constraint on the business.

___19 Our most senior IT person is as likely to become CEO as any (other) member of the board.

Name (optional): _____ Job title: _____

Department: _____ Date: _____

SCORING KEY

The scoring key in Figure A.5 shows the position that each question relates to on the pyramid. The shade of each level is determined by the total score achieved at that level, averaged over the number of respondents.

For example:

- Considering the bottom level (service delivery) of the pyramid first, say an IT function attained the maximum score of 7 on all six questions (numbering 10, 15, 12, 5, 4 and 14) this would give a total score of 42, and they would be in the white zone, i.e. 'cruising'.

- Considering the middle level (change agent) next, say an IT function attained a score of 5 on all seven questions (7, 17, 18, 13, 3, 16 and 1) this would give a total score of 35, and they would be in the pale grey zone, i.e. 'drifting'.

- Finally, considering the top level (business partner), say an IT function attained the minimum score of 1 on all six questions (9, 11, 8, 19, 6 and 2) this would give a total score of 6 and they would be in the dark grey zone, i.e. 'sinking'.

Figure A.5 Scoring key for IT health check

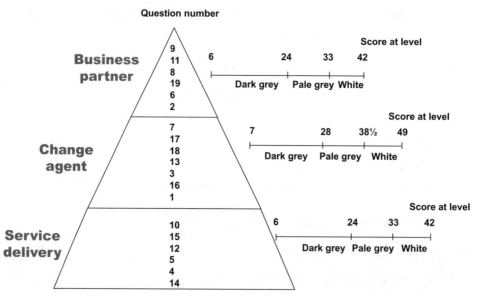

BENCHMARK

The data in Figure A.6 has been amassed from 62 different organisations over the past five years. You will find the average scores from 735 IT respondents (left pyramid) and 824 respondents from a variety of other business functions (right pyramid). Please use this data to compare yourself with the average and to track your progress over time.

Figure A.6 IT health check – benchmarking data

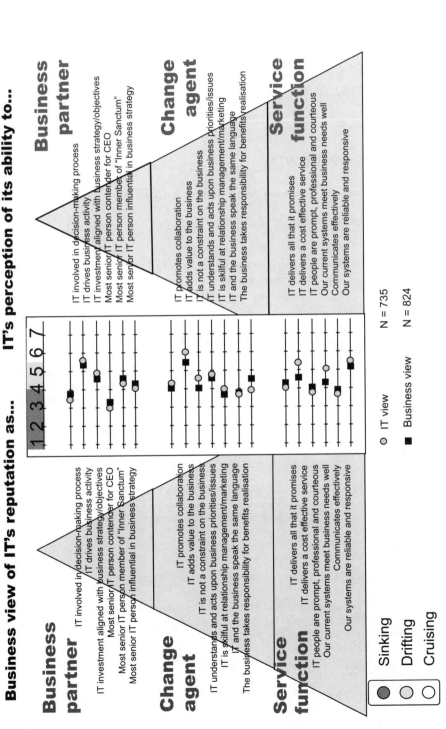

167

FURTHER READING

WHY IS THIS IMPORTANT?

I think the following two quotes sum it up very succinctly:

> The more I learn, the more I realize I don't know.
>
> Albert Einstein

> Anyone who stops learning is old, whether twenty or eighty. Anyone who keeps learning today is young. The greatest thing in life is to keep your mind young.
>
> Henry Ford

DELVING A LITTLE DEEPER INTO THE SUBJECT

Some people like to read books while others may prefer shorter articles and papers. You will find a list of suggested reading material in the following section that will hopefully cater for most tastes. It is categorised into subject areas so you may dip and dive at your leisure.

HINTS AND TIPS

The volume of reading material available to you is vast so you will need to be selective. I have selected a few of my choice books and papers as further food for thought. It is not a long list, as the saying goes 'sometimes less is more'.

Change

Kotter, J.P. (2006) *Our iceberg is melting*. London: Macmillan.

This is an easy read; simple and engaging. It is an ideal text to give to your team members to help them focus on the stages of change and the challenges of gaining wide acceptance that change needs to happen.

Kotter, J.P. (2008) *A sense of urgency*. Boston, MA: Harvard Business Press.

This book provides an explanation of the tactics that have been found to be effective in creating a sense of urgency during change initiatives. It also explores barriers to change and how to overcome them.

Communication

Dunning, D. (2003) *Introduction to type and communications*. Sunnyvale, CA: Consulting Psychologists Press.

This short, practical booklet examines how knowledge of your own and others' personality type can lead to more effective communication.

Emotional intelligence

Goleman, D. (1995) *Emotional intelligence*. New York: Bantam Books.

A very comprehensive text on the subject of emotional intelligence; a little hard going, but with plenty of examples.

Pease, A. (1995) *Body language: How to read others' thoughts by their gestures*. London: Sheldon Press.

An easy-to-read book that is both practical and insightful with lots of illustrations.

Human nature

Hallowell, E. (1999) The human moment at work. *Harvard Business Review*, (Jan/Feb). 58–66.

An enlightening paper providing insight into the brain chemistry behind face-to-face human interaction and how the absence of 'human moments' can wreak havoc in organisations.

Nicholson, N. (1998) How hardwired is human behaviour? *Harvard Business Review*, (Jul/Aug). 135–147.

An interesting insight into evolutionary psychology and our propensity to stereotype.

IT leadership

Chatham, R. and Sutton, B. (2010) *Changing the IT leader's mindset: Time for revolution rather than evolution*. Ely: IT Governance.

If you have your eye on a senior leadership position, this book will start you on your journey. Its focus is on transformational leadership, how to influence people and unite them in a common purpose to deliver a strategic vision.

Leadership – general

Collins, J. (2001) Level 5 leadership. *Harvard Business Review*, (Jan/Feb). 67–76.

An excellent insight into what makes a leader truly great – a paradoxical mixture of personal humility and professional will.

Kakabadse, A. (2010) *Facing up to the dark side of leadership*. Think: Cranfield. Available from: www.som.cranfield.ac.uk/som/p15716/think-cranfield/2010/november-2010/dark-side-of-leadership [August 2015].

An interesting insight into leadership when it goes wrong and the motives and drivers that can lead to 'bad leadership'.

Motivating people

Butler, T. and Waldroop, J. (1999) Job sculpting: The art of retaining your best people. *Harvard Business Review*, (Sept/Oct). 144–152.

An excellent paper providing both insight and practical advice in relation to motivating and developing people in the workplace.

Organisational politics

Patching, K. and Chatham, R. (2000) *Corporate politics for IT managers: How to get street-wise*. London: Butterworth Heinemann.

A good introduction to corporate politics written with the IT manager in mind but relevant to any discipline. It contains lots of cartoons to help develop your sense of humour.

Reputation

Sills, J. (2008) Becoming your own brand. *Psychology Today*, (Jan/Feb). Available from: www.psychologytoday.com/articles/200801/becoming-your-own-brand [August 2015].

A very short and punchy article that introduces the idea of managing your reputation as a personal brand.

Strategy

Hayashi, A. (2001) When to trust your gut. *Harvard Business Review at Large*, (Feb). 5–11.

A short but excellent article that provides insight into the process of strategic thinking with examples of 'out-of-the-box' thinking and practical advice as to how to sharpen your intuition.

Leonard, D. and Straus, S. (1997) Putting your company's whole brain to work. *Harvard Business Review*, (July/Aug). 111–121.

A well-constructed article focusing on the business imperative to innovate and how to harness the different thinking styles in a process of 'creative abrasion'.

Stress

Quenk, N. (2000) *In the grip; Understanding type, stress and the inferior function.* Oxford: OPP Ltd.

A short, but comprehensive, booklet that deals with the relationship between stress and personality type.

Systems and processes

Kim, G., Behr, K. and Spafford, G. (2014) *The phoenix project.* Portland, OR: IT Revolution Press.

A fast-paced, enlightening and entertaining novel about how to get out of the ITIL and MSP process mire and into DevOps.

Time management

Mankins, M., Brahm, C. and Caimi, G. (2014) Your scarcest resource. *Harvard Business Review*, (May/Jun). 1–8.

A fresh and insightful article that focuses on time as a scarce, but unmanaged resource. It describes how organisations squander time and how to establish organisation-wide time discipline.

Oncken, W. and Wass, D. (1974) Management time: Who's got the monkey? *Harvard Business Review*, (Nov/Dec).75–80.

One of the most impactful articles I have come across on the subject. The authors use a monkey analogy to highlight the issues of time management. Old, but just as relevant today as when it was written.

Work/life balance

Caproni, P. (2004) Work/life balance: You can't get there from here. *The Journal of Applied Behavioural Science*, 40(2). 208–218.

An insightful and fascinating article, written from the heart, offering a new perspective on the issue and illustrated with many personal examples.

Price, I. (2010) *The activity illusion.* Leicester: Matador.

An insight into why we work the way we do in the 21st century; why we live to work rather than work to live and what we can do to resolve the situation.

INDEX

7 Habits of Highly Effective People, The (Covey) 128

30-minute rule for tasks 130

80:20 rule, time management 130

active listening 20, 78, 117, 138, 148, 149

affective questions 150

ambivalence 34

analytical questions 150

appraisals 16, 18

aspirational needs 6

assertiveness 139

attitude
    maintaining positive 134–6
    performance issues 21–3, 26

attributes for leadership 91–2

baboons, political zoo 114, 115, 116, 117

Baddeley, Simon 114

beginners, directing and guiding 11–12

believable and compelling messages 54–5

belonging, need for sense of 102

benchmarking, IT health check 166, 167

benefits versus features of IT 63–4

big picture versus detail 46

body language 137, 140–1

boss (your)
    bullying from 120–3
    getting to know 72
    getting feedback from 73
    giving feedback to 73–4
    management style 72

    managing 70–4
    seeking coaching from 73
    trust and loyalty 74

bouncers, type of bully 121, 123

brand image, personal 110–11

brutes, type of bully 121, 123

budgets 82, 85

bullying behaviour 120–3

business partner, level of IT function 163, 164, 166, 167

Butler, T. 136

capabilities 91–2

capability and attitude, performance 21–3

capable people, exciting and empowering 12–13

change agent 163, 164, 166

change curve 34, 35

change initiatives, strategic thinking 38

change leadership 33–7

Clarke, Arthur C. 88

classification of others 107–8

clean questions 65

cleverness, bullies 121

closed questions 65

coaching
    choosing a coach 147
    fallen angels 26
    problem children 25
    rising stars 26
    role models 27
    seeking from your boss 73
    skills 148–52

collaboration 139

comedy 154, 155

common interests 72, 77, 141

common sense 85

communication skills 45–52
    influencing people 53–5
    presentation skills 56–61
    report writing 61–2
    talking to customers 63–6
    see also email; feedback

competitor intelligence 87

complementary skills, team members 29

compromising versus collaboration 139

concentration 129
    hints and tips 129
    when listening to others 138

confidence versus arrogance 141

conflict situations, political zoo 116

consistency of words and actions 111

consultants, credibility of 68

control mechanisms 84

corporate politics 113–19

cortisol and stress 96–7

counselling, life interest 136

Covey, S. 128

creativity 87–8
    life interest 136

credibility 58, 68

cultural awareness 141

customer understanding 63–6, 160

cyber security 88

Deal, Terrence E. 143
decision-making
    delegating 13
    by different personality types 46–7, 48
decisiveness 130
deeply embedded life interests (DELIs) 136–7
delegation 9–14
    challenges 129
    hints and tips 10–13
    importance of 9–10
    psychological barriers 10
DELIs (deeply embedded life interests) 136–7
delivery 162
detail versus big picture 46
development, personal 145–7
    feedback providing 15, 17
dialogue, promoting open 50, 73
difference, handling 139
digital era, impact of IT in 86–8
'direction' of low skill/low will people, delegation 11–12
dirty questions 65
dolphin, political zoo 114
    5 important things to do 117
    behaviour in various situations 116–17
    characteristics of 115–16
drive versus stress 97

easy tasks, beginning with 36
eating healthily 106, 129, 135
effectiveness 127
efficiency 127
email
    addiction survey 100
    rules of effective 52
    time management issues 128–9, 130
    using appropriately 131
emotional intelligence (EQ) 132–41
    emotions, managing 132, 133–6
    empathy 133, 137–8
    focus 132, 136–7
    self-awareness 132, 133
    social skill 133, 138–41
    status 141
emotions
    and the change curve 34
    humour-related 153–5

managing own 132, 133–6
understanding others' 133, 137–8
empathy towards others 133, 137–8
    active listening 149
    sociable type 50
'empower' high skill/high will people, delegation 11, 13
encouragement
    of others' ideas 138–9
    of teamwork 31–2
    when giving feedback 17
enterprise control, life interest 137
enthusiastic beginners, guiding 12
essential management skills 3–41
    change leadership 33–7
    delegation 9–14
    feedback 15–20
    good managers 3–8
    performance issues 21–7
    strategic thinking 38–41
    team development 28–32
esteem, need for 102
estimation skills 85
ex-peers/colleagues, managing 91–3
'excite' high skill/low will people, delegation 11, 12–13
excuses, removing 35
executive summary, reports 61–2
exercise/physical activity 97, 98, 99, 106, 135
experienced colleagues, managing 91–3
experiences, broadening 146–7
explorative questions 151

facial expressions, reading 137, 140
failure, using as a learning opportunity 135
'fallen angels' 22, 23
    dealing with 26
family time, finding 106
feedback
    asking for 17, 19–20
    asking from your boss 73
    constructive 148, 149
    giving 15–16, 17–18

giving to your boss 73–4
helpful and unhelpful 18, 19
importance of 15
receiving 17, 20
feelings see emotions
Ferrari, teamwork 29
first impressions 108–10
'fit for purpose', project control 82
focus, emotional intelligence 132
    life interests 136–7
foxes, political zoo 114, 115, 116
    dealing with 117–19
fresh questions 151
fulfilment 101, 102, 103

generosity 78, 94, 117, 143–4
goals, GROW model 149, 151
GROW (goals, reality, options, wrap up) model 149
'growing up', letting go of jobs you like doing 94–5, 129
'guiding' low skill/high will people 11, 12

health check see IT health check
high-potential projects 83, 84
honesty 55, 131
hours spent working 101, 102–3, 106
human-to-human contact, benefits of 102
humour 135, 141, 153–5

idealistic types 46, 47
    communicating with 48, 49
    influencing 54
    presenting to 59
ideas
    of others, building upon 138–9
    questions generating new 151
    and thoughts, connections between 139
influencing skills 53–5
    life interest 137
integrity, acting with 114, 115
intelligence see emotional intelligence (EQ)
interpersonal skills
    networking 111–12
    relationship management 75–8
IT function, 3 levels of 162–3

IT health check 162–7
  benchmarking data 166–7
  example output from 164
  questionnaire 163, 165
  scoring key for 166
IT potential, harnessing 87–8
IT stereotype 107–10

James, Kim 114
jargon, avoiding 62, 64
jokes 154
Jung, Carl 46

Kennedy, Alan A. 143
key operational projects 83
Kissinger, Henry 53
knowledge
  gaining new 138, 147
  and organisational politics 114
  systems and processes 81–5
  technical 86–8
Kotter, J.P. 33
Kübler-Ross, Elizabeth 34

laughter 6, 153
leadership
  for change 33–7
  qualities 3–4, 91–2, 156–7
  rotating, teamwork 29
learning
  the art of managing 145–6
  from listening 117
  mindset, developing 146–7
  to say no 131
leisure time 102–3, 106
'letting go' of jobs 94–5
life interests 136–7
life purpose, articulating 103–6
likeability 109–10, 154
listening skills 20, 78, 117, 138, 148, 149
loyalty
  building with others 142–4
  with your boss 74

malevolent intent, bullying 120
malice, intended versus unintended 122–3
management issues/problems 91–123

bullying 120–3
letting go 94–5
managing ex-peers/older people 91–3
politics 113–19
reputation 107–12
stress and pressure 96–9
work/life balance 100–6
management skills
  communication 45–52
  customer understanding 63–6
  influencing people 53–5
  managing your boss 70–4
  relationship management 75–8
  reports and presentations 56–62
  supplier negotiations 67–9
  see also essential management skills
managers
  failure to delegate 9–10
  first 90 days 158–67
  leadership rules 4–5
Maslow's hierarchy of needs 101–2, 103
'me' time 106, 136
mental status 141
mentoring, life interest 136
mentors 146–7
messages
  believable and compelling 54–5
  email 52
  medium for and purpose of 51
  reinforced by body language 140
methodologies, knowledge of 81
mirroring 140
modelling of behaviour 31, 162
motivation
  to change 35
  coaching skills 148–52
  life interests 136–7
  Maslow's hierarchy of needs 101–2, 103
  of team members 4–5
  see also feedback

needs
  communication 46
  of customers 64

Maslow's hierarchy 101–2, 103
  of your team 6
negative attitude
  fallen angels 23
  problem children 22
  ways to avoid 134–6
negotiations with suppliers 69
nervous beginners, directing 11–12
networking 111–12
neuronal groups, concept clusters 108
non-verbal cues/signals, reading 133, 137
note-making, one-place system 130–1
nutrition 106, 129, 135

objectives
  coaching 151, 152
  and the four 'types' of people 46–7
  for your first 90 days 158
On Death and Dying (Kübler-Ross) 34
one-place system for recording notes 130–1
open dialogue, promoting 50
open questions 50, 65, 146
openness 72–3
options, GROW model 149, 152
organisation, of oneself 130–1
organisational change 33–7
organisational politics 113–19
outcome-focused thinking 39

Pareto Principle 130
partnership relations with suppliers 68
peer pressure, teams 35
people skills see emotional intelligence (EQ)
perfectionism 154
performance
  dealing with poor 21–7
  effect of stress on 96–7
personal brand image 110–11
personal development 145–7
personal needs of your team 6
personal values 104–5
  articulating 105–6
  rebalancing 106

personality type 46–7
    communication style to use with different 47–50
    presentation style to use with different 57–60
    of your boss 72
physical activity/exercise 97, 98, 99, 106, 135
physical well-being 135–6
pilot analogy, project management 82
place, for communicating 51
planned networking 112
planning your day 130–1
political zoo 114–16
politics, organisational 113–19
poor performance, dealing with 21–7
positive outlook, maintaining 134–6
pragmatic types 46
    communicating with 48, 49
    influencing 54
    presenting to 57
praise 13, 78, 143
presentation skills 56–61
pressure, coping with 96–9
prioritising opportunities 162
priority matrix 128
probing questions 150
'problem children' 22
    dealing with 25
    problems
    long-term performance 25
    treat as learning opportunity 133–4
processes and systems 81–5
procrastination, avoiding 130
project management 82
project types 82–4
psychological barriers to delegation 10
psychological types, Jung 46–7
psychometric instruments 30–1, 133
public recognition 143
purpose
    'fit for purpose', project control 82
    life purpose 103–6
    of your communication 51

qualities for leadership 91–2
quantitative analysis, life interest 136
questions, asking
    coaching skills 26, 148, 150–1, 152
    customers 65–6
    learning opportunities 146
    and social skill development 138

RACE (relationship building, active listening, constructive feedback, effective questioning) 148, 149–51
ranking of employees 32
reality, GROW model 149, 152
reflective questions 150
relationship building 5, 76–7, 148, 149
relationship management 75–8
    life interest 137
relaxation 136
report writing 56, 61–2
reputation, managing and enhancing 107–12
requirements, ascertaining 64–5
'resisters', dealing with 36
respect 5, 75, 78, 102
'rising stars' 22–3
    dealing with 25–6
risk management 82
role modelling of behaviour 31, 162
'role models' 23
    dealing with 27
'runaway trains', bullies 121, 123

schemers 121
    dealing with 123
security, need for 101, 102
self-awareness, emotional intelligence 132
    developing 133
self-control, bullies 121
self-organisation 130–1
service delivery, level of IT function 163, 164, 166, 167
shared purpose, teams 29
sheep, political zoo 114, 115, 116, 117
skill versus will matrix 11–13
skills for leadership 91–2

sleep, getting sufficient 106, 136
'so what' test 61
sociable types 46, 47, 48
    communicating with 50
    influencing 54
    presenting to 59–60
social media 101–2, 111
social skill, emotional intelligence 133
    active listening 138
    body language 140–1
    building on others' ideas 138–9
    handling difference 139
    questioning 138
    social connections 141
    status 141
status 141
stereotyping of IT people 107
    key characteristics 108–9
    ways of opposing 109–10
storytelling, life interest 137
strategic projects 83
strategic thinking 38–41
stress 96–9
    avoidance of 97–8
    effect on performance 96–7
    of others, dealing with 99
    recognising signs of 98
    remedies for 98–9
success, celebration of 36
supplier relationships 67–9
support projects 83, 84
supportive actions 6–7, 35
survival 102
systems 81–5
systems analysis 161

tasks
    30-minute rule 130
    delegating 9–14, 129
    handling 131
    urgent versus important 127–8
team-building events 30–1
team development 28–32
team players 30
team relationship building 5
teams, features of 28–9
technical knowledge 86–8
technological capabilities 87

technology, life interest 136
theoretical types 46
  communicating with 48, 49
  influencing 54
  presenting to 57–8
theorising, life interest 136
time management 127–31
time out, taking 98, 134–5
time thieves, banishing 128–9
timing of communication 51
TLC (tender loving care) 137–8
tone
  of email messages 52
  of voice 65, 141
tools 125–55
  coaching skills 148–52
  emotional intelligence
  132–41

humour 153–5
  personal development
  145–7
  time management 127–31
  trust and loyalty 142–4
training 25, 26, 35, 145–7
transparency 73
trust 117
  building with your boss 74
  and delegation 71
  engendering from others
  142–4
truthfulness 35, 50, 140

urgency 33, 127–8

value proposition 68
values, personal 104–6

vision 87
vocal status 141

Waldroop, J. 136
wants versus needs of
customers 64
wasted time, eliminating 130
'weisure' time 100–1
well-being 135–6
will versus skill matrix 11
win-win strategies 117, 138,
139
work/life balance 100–6
working hours 101, 102–3, 106
wrap up, GROW model 149, 152

zone of death 161
zoo, political 114–16